United States
Department of
Agriculture

Forest Service

Northern
Research Station

Resource Bulletin
NRS-41

Michigan's Forests, 2004: Statistics and Quality Assurance

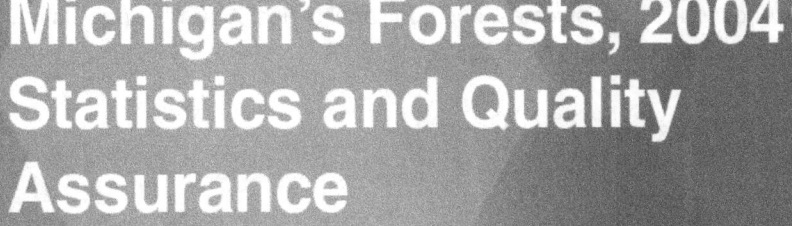

Scott A. Pugh, Mark H. Hansen, Gary Brand, and
Ronald E. McRoberts

Abstract

The first annual inventory of Michigan's forests was completed in 2004 after 18,916 plots were selected and 10,355 forested plots were visited. This report includes detailed information on forest inventory methods, quality of estimates, and additional tables. An earlier publication presented analyses of the inventoried data (Pugh et al. 2009).

The Authors

SCOTT A. PUGH is a forester with the Forest Inventory and Analysis program, Northern Research Station, St. Paul, MN.

MARK H. HANSEN is a research associate with the University of Minnesota, Department of Forest Resources, St. Paul, MN.

GARY BRAND is a computer systems analyst with the University of Nevada, Las Vegas, NV.

RONALD E. MCROBERTS is a mathematical statistician with the Forest Inventory and Analysis program, Northern Research Station, St. Paul, MN.

CONTENTS

FOREST INVENTORY METHODS
Strategic Model

The Forest Inventory and Analysis (FIA) program of the U.S. Forest Service's Northern Research Station is part of the national enhanced FIA program that focuses on a set of six strategic objectives (McRoberts 2005):

- A standard set of variables with nationally consistent meanings and measurements
- Field inventories of all forested lands
- Nationally consistent estimation
- Adherence to national precision standards
- Consistent reporting and data distribution
- Credibility with users and stakeholders

To ensure that these objectives are achieved, 10 strategic approaches have been prescribed:

- A national set of prescribed core variables with a national field manual that describes measurement procedures and protocols for each variable.
- A national plot configuration
- A nationally consistent sampling design
- Estimation using standardized formulae for sample-based estimators
- A national database of FIA data with core standards and user-friendly public access
- A national information management system
- A nationally consistent set of tables with estimates of prescribed core variables
- Publication of statewide tables with estimates of prescribed core variables at 5-year intervals
- Documentation of the technical aspects of the FIA program including procedures, protocols, and techniques
- Peer review and publication of the technical documentation for general access

The result of the strategic objectives and approaches is an inventory program with identifiably new features and a nationally consistent plot configuration, a nationally consistent sampling design for all lands, annual measurement of a proportion of plots in each state, nationally consistent estimation techniques and algorithms, and integration of the ground-sampling components of the FIA inventory and detection monitoring by the U.S. Forest Service's Forest Health Monitoring (FHM) program.

Plot Configuration

The national FIA plot design (Fig. 1) consists of four 24-ft-radius subplots configured as a central subplot and three peripheral subplots. Centers of the peripheral subplots are located 120 ft from the central subplot and at azimuths of 360, 120, and 240 degrees from the center of the central subplot. Each tree with diameter at breast height (d.b.h.) 5 inches or greater is measured on these subplots. Each subplot contains a 6.8-ft-radius microplot with center located 12 ft east of the subplot center on which each tree with d.b.h. between 1 and 5 inches is measured. Forest conditions that occur on any of the four subplots are identified and recorded; if the area of the condition is 1 acre or greater, the condition is mapped on the subplot. Factors that differentiate forest conditions include forest type, stand-size class, stand origin, land use, ownership, and density. Macroplots are not used by the Northern Research Station but Rocky Mountain and Pacific Northwest Research Stations use these larger sample areas in some cases. Macroplots have a radius of 58.9 feet and are used for sampling intensification or sampling relatively rare events.

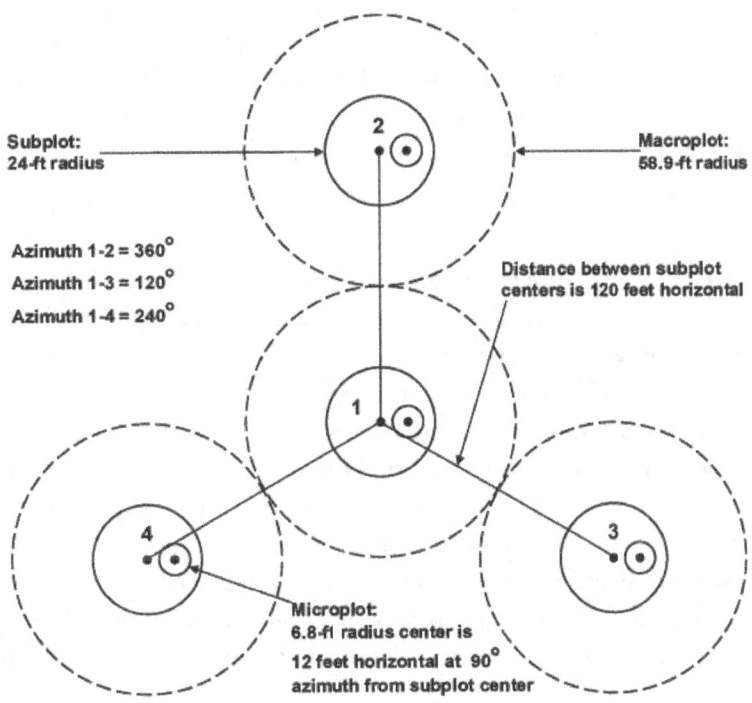

Figure 1.   National FIA plot design (adapted from Bechtold and Patterson 2005).

Sample Design

Historic sampling errors indicate that a sampling intensity of about one plot per 6,000 acres is required to satisfy national FIA precision guidelines. Therefore, FIA divided the area of the United States into nonoverlapping, 5,937-acre hexagons and established a plot in each hexagon as follows: 1) if an existing FHM plot was located in a hexagon, it was selected; 2) if there was no FHM plot in the hexagon, the existing FIA plot from the previous periodic inventory nearest the hexagon center was selected; and 3) if neither an FHM nor an FIA plot was located in the hexagon, a new FIA plot was established at a random location in the hexagon (Brand et al. 2000, McRoberts 1999). This array of field plots is designated the Federal base sample and is considered an equal probability sample; its measurement is funded by the Federal government.

The Federal base sample was divided into five interpenetrating, nonoverlapping panels or subsamples, each of which provides complete, systematic coverage of a state. Each year, plots of a single panel are measured and panels are selected on a 5-year, rotating basis (McRoberts 1999). For estimation purposes, the measurement of each panel of plots is considered an independent, equal probability sample of all lands in a state.

Three-phase Inventory

FIA conducts inventories in three phases. Phase 1 uses remotely sensed data to obtain initial plot land-cover observations and to stratify land area in the population of interest to increase the precision of estimates. In Phase 2, field crews visit the physical locations of permanent field plots to measure traditional inventory variables such as tree species, diameter, and height. In Phase 3, field crews visit a subset of Phase 2 plots to obtain measurements for an additional suite of variables associated with forest and ecosystem health. The three phases of the enhanced FIA program as implemented in this inventory are discussed in greater detail in the sections that follow.

Phase 1

Aerial photographs, digital orthoquads (DOQs: digitally scanned aerial photograph), and satellite imagery are used for initial plot measurement via remotely sensed data and stratification. Phase 1 plot measurement consists of observations of conditions at the plot locations using aerial photographs or DOQs. Analysts determine a digitized geographic location for each field plot and a human interpreter assigns the plot a land cover/use based on these observations. Lands satisfying FIA's definition of forest land include commercial timberland, some pastured land with trees, forest plantations, unproductive forested land, and reserved, noncommercial forested land. In addition, forest land requires minimum stocking levels, a 1-acre minimum area, and a minimum bole-to-bole width of 120 ft with continuous canopy. Forest land excludes wooded strips and windbreaks less than 120 feet wide and idle farmland or other previously nonforest land that currently is below minimum stocking levels. All plot locations that could possibly contain accessible forest land are selected for further measurement during Phase 2.

The combination of natural variability among plots and budgetary constraints prohibits measurement of a sufficient number of plots to satisfy national precision standards for most inventory variables unless the estimation process is enhanced using ancillary data. Thus, the land area is stratified by using remotely sensed data to facilitate stratified estimation.

A stratification scheme based on satellite imagery as proposed by Hansen and Wendt (2000) is applied to the National Land Cover Data (NLCD) as suggested by McRoberts et al. (2002). The NLCD is a digital land-cover map of the conterminous United States in which 30- by 30-m pixels are assigned to 21 land-cover classes. The land-cover classification was produced by the U.S. Geological Survey and was based on nominal 1992 Landsat 5 Thematic Mapper (TM) satellite imagery and a variety of ancillary data (Vogelmann et al. 2001). Four strata are created using a three-step process: 1) aggregate NLCD classes with trees into a forest stratum with the remaining classes into a nonforest stratum; 2) reclassify isolated groups of three or fewer pixels into their surrounding forest or nonforest class to comply with the FIA criterion that forest land must be at least 1 acre; and 3) create two additional classes (forest edge and nonforest edge) that includes all pixels within two pixels of the forest/nonforest boundary.

In addition to classifying every pixel into one of the four strata, every pixel is assigned to an ownership strata based on the Protected Areas Database (PAD) described by DellaSala et al. (2001). In Michigan, PAD was used to classify pixels into three ownership classes: 1) national forest (2,840,000 acres); 2) other public owners (4,865,000 acres); and 3) private owners (29,639,000 acres). Every pixel also was assigned to a county based on the location of the pixel center.

Stratified estimation requires that two tasks be accomplished. First, each plot must be assigned to a single stratum. Next, the proportion of each detailed stratum must be calculated (TM land-cover classification, ownership, and county group delineation). The first task is accomplished by assigning each plot to the stratum assigned to the pixel containing the center of the center subplot. The second task is accomplished by calculating the proportion of pixels in each stratum. The population estimate for a variable is calculated as the sum across all strata of the product of each stratum's observed proportion (from Phase 1) and the variable's estimated mean per unit area for the stratum (from Phase 2). Details of the stratum assignments used in Michigan are presented in the estimation section of this report that follows the Phase 2 and Phase 3 descriptions.

Phase 2

In Phase 2, field crews record a variety of data for plot locations previously determined in Phase 1 to be accessible forest land. Before visiting plot locations, field crews consult county land records to determine the ownership of plots and then seek permission from private landowners to measure plots on their lands. Field crews determine the location of the geographic center of the center subplot using geographic positioning system (GPS) receivers. They record condition-level observations that include land-cover, forest type, stand origin, stand age, stand-size class, site-productivity class, history of forest disturbance, and land use for every condition (major land use or forest stand at least 1 acre in size) that occurs on the plot. They also record information on condition boundaries when multiple conditions are found on a plot. For each tree, field crews record a variety of observations and measurements, including condition, species, live/dead status, lean, diameter, height, crown ratio (percent of tree height represented by crown), crown class (dominant, codominant, suppressed), damage, and decay status. Office staff use statistical models based on field crew measurements to calculate values for additional variables, including individual-tree volume, per unit area estimates of number of trees, volume, and biomass by plot, condition, species group, and live/dead status. Details of the data collection procedures used in Phase 2 are available at http://www.nrs.fs.fed.us/fia/data-collection/.

Phase 3

The third phase of the enhanced FIA program focuses on forest health. Phase 3 is administered by the FIA program with consultation from other Forest Service programs such as the FHM program, other Federal agencies, state natural resource agencies, and universities. The FHM program consists of four interrelated and complementary activities: detection, evaluation and intensive site-ecosystem monitoring, and research on monitoring techniques. Detection monitoring consists of systematic aerial and ground surveys designed to collect baseline information on the current condition of forest ecosystems and to detect changes from those baselines over time. Evaluation monitoring studies examine the extent, severity, and probable causes of changes in forest health identified through the detection monitoring surveys. Intensive site-ecosystem monitoring studies regionally specific ecological processes at a network of sites located in representative forested ecosystems. Research on monitoring techniques focuses on developing and refining indicator measurements to improve the efficiency and reliability of data collection and analysis at all levels of the program.

The ground survey portion of the detection monitoring program was integrated into the FIA program as Phase 3 in 1999. The Phase 3 sample consists of a 1:16 subset of the Phase 2 plots with one Phase 3 plot for about every 95,000 acres. Phase 3 measurements are obtained by field crews during the growing season and include an extended suite of ecological data: lichen diversity and abundance, soil quality (erosion, compaction, and chemistry), vegetation diversity and structure, and down woody material. The incidence and severity of ozone injury for selected bioindicator species also are monitored as part of an associated sampling scheme. All Phase 2 measurements are collected on each Phase 3 plot at the same time as the Phase 3 measurements. Additional information on the collection procedures used in Phase 3 is available at http://www.nrs.fs.fed.us/fia/topics/.

Phase 3 variables are selected to address specific criteria outlined by the Montreal Process Working Group for the conservation and sustainable management of temperate and boreal forests and are based on the concept of indicator variables. Observations of an indicator variable represent an index of ecosystem functions that can be monitored over time to assess trends. Indicator variables are used in conjunction with each other, Phase 2 data, data from FHM evaluation monitoring studies, and ancillary data to address ecological issues such as vegetation diversity, fuel loading, regional air-quality gradients, and carbon storage. The Phase 2 and Phase 3 data of the enhanced FIA program are a primary source of reporting data for the Montreal Process criteria.

Estimation

Most of the estimates and analysis of forest resources presented in this report, including all of the estimates in Tables 1 through 61, are based on data observed on the 18,916 Phase 2 plots across Michigan (Fig. 2). The analysis of forest health issues that relate to down woody materials, soils, ozone damage, and crown condition are based on data observed on the 398 Phase 3 plots (Fig 3).

Approximately 20 percent of the Phase 2 observations were acquired each year from October 1, 1999 thru September 30, 2004. These observations are collectively called the 2004 inventory. These plots are located within 41 estimation strata (Table A) defined by combinations of the four Phase 1 classes (nonforest, nonforest edge, forest edge, and forest), a land-ownership classification created from the PAD and county groups. Procedures described in Bechtold and Patterson (2005) for stratified estimation with observed stratum areas were used in conjunction with the strata in Table A to produce all estimates. Table A shows the total area and number of plots within each stratum.

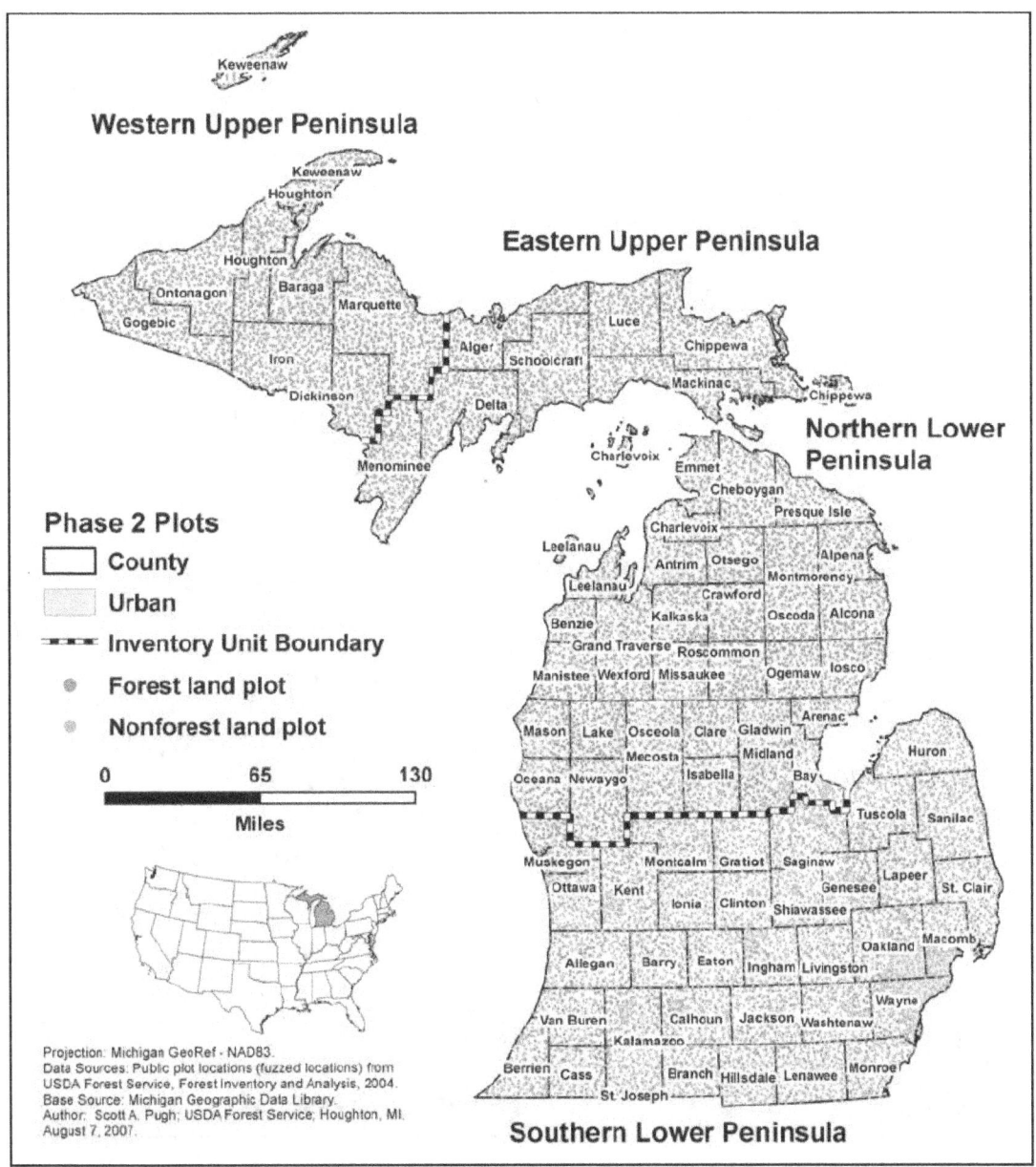

Figure 2. Approximate locations of the 18,916 forest and nonforest land Phase 2 plots, Michigan, 2004.

Integration with Previous Inventories

In 2004, FIA completed measurement of the fifth panel of inventory plots in Michigan. The 2004 panel, along with those surveyed in 2000, 2001, 2002 and 2003, completed data collection for the fifth inventory of Michigan's forests (Pugh et al. 2009), the 2004 inventory. Previous inventories of Michigan's forest resources were completed in 1935 (Lake States For. Exp. Stn. 1936), 1955 (Findell et al. 1960), 1966 (Chase et al. 1970), 1980 (Raile and Smith 1983, Spencer 1983), and 1993 (Leatherberry and Spencer 1996, Schmidt et al. 1997). Data from new inventories often are compared with data from earlier inventories to determine trends in forest resources. However, for the comparisons to be valid, the procedures used in the two inventories must be similar.

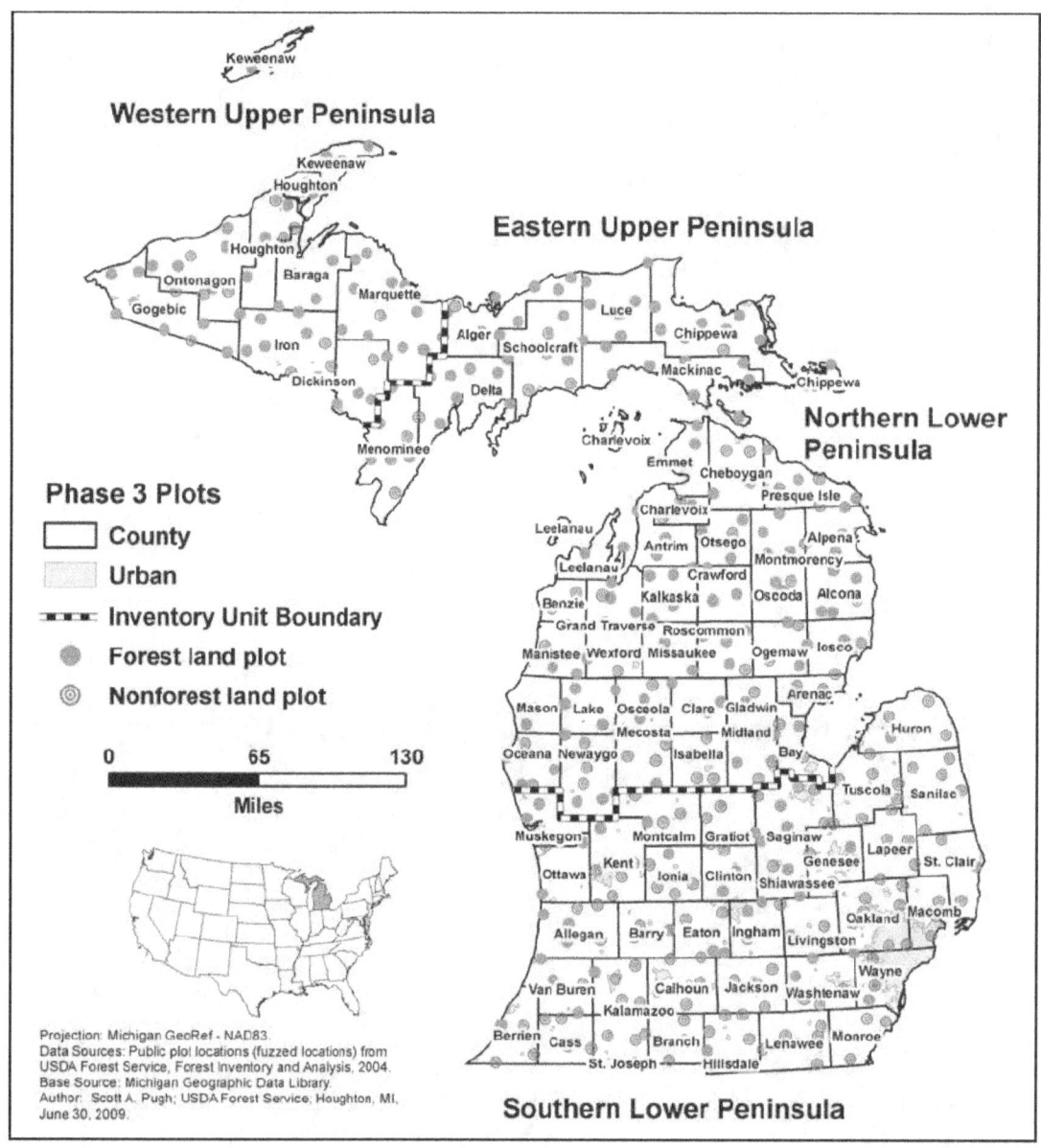

Figure 3.   Approximate locations of the 398 forest and nonforest land Phase 3 plots, Michigan, 2004.

To improve the consistency, efficiency, and reliability of the inventory, a number of major changes occurred between the 1993 and 2004 inventories. For example, some land-use classes are considered forest in this 2004 inventory but they were nonforest in the 1993 inventory. Also, the minimum stocking (relative density of trees) percentage for forest land changed from 16.7 in the 1993 inventory to 10 percent in the 2004 inventory. These changes had virtually no effect on forest and timberland estimates.

There were greater changes in stocking, forest-type, and stand-size estimates. Methods for calculating stocking were improved in the 2004 inventory. Forest type and stand size are determined from stocking, and more precise definitions of forest type were developed for the 2004 inventory. For additional information on stocking, see "National Algorithms for Determining Stocking Class, Stand Size Class, and Forest Type for Forest Inventory and Analysis Plots" (Arner et al. 2003).

The new forest-type definitions follow a national standard and designate more precise types. This standard provides consistency at the national level but is inconsistent with some previous regional classifications. After reclassifying the 1993 inventory using the 2004 methods, some classifications changed to white pine/hemlock, eastern hemlock, eastern redcedar, oak/pine, oak/gum/cypress, other exotic hardwoods, and a few other softwood types that were not previously valid (Table B). The new definitions also resulted in some classifications that do not exist at the local level. For example 56,600 acres (30 plots) were classified as sweetbay/swamp tupelo/red maple (member of oak/gum/cypress forest-type group). Michigan is outside the range of sweetbay/swamp tupelo/red maple. This issue occurs in wet conditions where red maple is the dominant species. These areas would be more appropriately classified as red maple/lowland.

Using the 2004 methods with the 1993 data, more acreage was classified as poletimber and less as seedling/sapling and sawtimber (Table C). There were also modeled plots used in the 1993 inventory. These modeled plots generally resulted in an overestimation in the size of trees. Revising estimates after removing modeled plots further reduces the 1993 estimate of sawtimber acreage and increases the poletimber estimate. Using the revised methods with no modeled plots for 1993, the acreage of sawtimber drops 32 percent, from 8.6 to 5.8 million, and poletimber increases 52 percent, from 5.5 to 8.4 million acres.

Some variables such as site productivity were assigned to modeled plots in 1993 using values from the 1980 inventory. The methods used to assign site productivity in 1980 varied from those used on measured plots in the 1993 and 2004 inventories. Therefore, apparent changes in site productivity from 1993 to 2004 are questionable. Given the issues with modeled plots the practice was discontinued. For additional information on the effects of modeled plots in the 1993 inventory see Pugh et al. (2009).

New methods were used to calculate average annual net growth of growing stock in the 2004 inventory. In this report, these new methods were adjusted to make estimates of the 2004 inventory more comparable with other inventories (Tables 24, 60, and 65). Previously published estimates for the 2004 inventory (Hansen and Brand 2006) added the entire volume of a tree to growing-stock net growth if the tree changed from nongrowing stock or cull in the previous inventory of 1993 to growing stock in the current inventory of 2004. The entire volume of the tree was subtracted from the estimate if it changed from growing stock to cull. Using the adjusted methods in this report, only the growth of a tree from the previous inventory to the current inventory is added or subtracted from growing-stock net growth. This modification is an improvement, more in line with inventories from other years. The updated estimate (786.8 million ft^3) of average annual net growth of growing stock on timberland is 15 percent less than the previously published estimate (923.3 million ft^3).

A major change between the two inventories was the change in plot design. For the sake of consistency, a new, national plot design was implemented by all five regional FIA units in 1999. Prior to this new plot design, fixed and variable-radius subplots were used in the 1980 and 1993 inventories. The new design uses fixed-radius subplots exclusively. Both designs have strong points but they often produce different classifications for individual plot characteristics. Unpublished FIA research comparing these plot designs showed no noticeable difference in volume and tree-count estimates.

For additional information on the sample protocols and estimation procedures for the first two phases of the FIA program, see Bechtold and Patterson (2005). For additional information on Phase 3 indicator sampling protocols, see USDA For. Serv. (2003) and Woodall and Monleon (2008).

COMMON SOURCES OF ERROR

There are two general types of error, random variability (precision) and estimation bias (accuracy). Random variability refers to the precision of the estimate, which would occur if the entire sampling and estimation process were to be repeated many times. Estimation bias, refers to the difference between the estimate and the "true value" in the absence of this random variability and refers to the overestimation or underestimation inherent in the entire estimation process.

Errors in the estimates presented in this report (both random variability and estimation bias) are affected by various sources. The four primary sources of error common to all sample-based estimates are sampling, measurement, prediction, and nonresponse error. A section is devoted to each of these sources of error. Included in each section is a definition of the source of error in the context of the FIA inventory as well as a discussion of methods used to quantify and/or reduce that source of error. Measures of sampling, measurement, and prediction errors associated with various attributes are presented. Issues of possible bias related to nonresponse also are addressed.

Sampling Error

The process of sampling (selecting a random subset of a population and calculating estimates from this subset) causes estimates to contain error they would not have if every member of the population (e.g., every tree in the State) had been observed and included in the sample. The 2004 inventory of Michigan is based on a sample of 18,916 plots located randomly across the State (total area of 37.3 million acres), or a sampling rate of about one plot for every 2,000 acres.

The procedures for statistical estimation outlined in the previous section and described in detail in Bechtold and Patterson (2005) provide the estimates of the population totals and means presented in this report. Along with every estimate is an associated sampling error that is typically expressed as a percentage of the estimated value (the estimated value plus or minus the sampling error). This sampling error is the primary measure of the reliability of an estimate. This report utilizes a sampling error based on one standard error, which means the chances are two in three that had a 100 percent inventory been taken using these methods, the results would have been within the limits indicated.

The sampling errors for State-level estimates of the major attributes presented in this report are presented in Table D. Table 65 presents sampling errors for these estimates at the FIA inventory unit and county levels.

Estimates for classifications smaller than the State totals in Table D will have larger sampling errors. For example, Table 65 shows the sampling error for timberland area in any county is higher than that for total timberland area in the State. To compute an approximate sampling error for an estimate that is smaller than a State total, use the following formula:

$$E = \frac{(SE)\sqrt{(\text{State total estimate})}}{\sqrt{(\text{Smaller estimate})}} \qquad (1)$$

where:

E = approximate sampling error for smaller estimate

SE = sampling error for State total estimate (percent)

For example, to compute the error on the area of forest land in the oak/hickory forest-type group for the State, proceed as follows:

The total area of the oak/hickory group in the State from Table 3 is 2.6 million acres.

The total area of all forest land in the State from Table 3 is 19.3 million acres.

The State total error for forest land area from Table D is 0.37 percent.

Using formula (1):

$$\text{Sampling error} = E = \frac{(0.37)\sqrt{(19.3)}}{\sqrt{(2.6)}} = 1.0 \text{ percent.}$$

This approximation works well for estimates of area, volume, number of trees, and biomass. It is less effective for estimates of growth, removals, or mortality. Individuals seeking more accurate sampling errors should use Forest Inventory Data Online (FIDO), available at http://fiatools.fs.fed.us.

The estimators used by FIA are unbiased under the assumptions that the sample plots are a random sample of the total population and the observed value for any plot is the true value for that plot. Deviations from these basic assumptions are not reflected in the computation of sampling errors. The following sections on measurement, prediction, and nonresponse error address possible departures from these basic assumptions.

Measurement Error

Errors associated with the methods and instruments used to observe and record the sample attributes are called measurement errors. On FIA plots, attributes such as the diameter and height of a tree are measured with different instruments. Other attributes such as species and crown class are observed without the aid of an instrument. On a typical FIA plot, 30 to 70 trees are observed with 15 to 20 attributes recorded on each tree. Also, many attributes that describe the plot and conditions on the plot are observed. Errors in any of these observations affect the quality of the estimates. If a measurement is biased (such as tree diameter consistently taken at an incorrect place on the tree), the estimates that use this observation (such as volume) will reflect this bias. Even if measurements are unbiased, high levels of random error in the measurements will add to the total random error of the estimation process.

To ensure that all FIA observations are made to the highest standards possible, a regular program of quality control and quality assurance is an integral part of all FIA data-collection efforts. This program begins with the documentation of protocols and procedures used in the inventory followed by extensive crew training. To assess the quality of the data collected by these trained crews, a random sample of at least 4 percent of all plots is measured independently by a different qualified crew. These independent measurements are referred to as blind checks, the purpose of which is to assess the quality of field measurements. A second measurement on blind check plots is made by a quality assurance (QA) crew. QA crews have as much or more experience and training in FIA field measurements as that of standard FIA crews.

The quality of field measurements is assessed nationally through a set of measurement quality objectives (MQOs) that are set for every data item collected. Each MQO consists of two parts: a tolerance or acceptable level of measurement error and an objective in terms of the percent of measurements within tolerance. Blind check measurements are used to observe how often individual field crews are meeting these objectives and to assess the overall compliance among all crews. Table E shows the compliance rates for various measurements used to compute the estimates included in this report and in other FIA reports. Columns labeled "Michigan" are based on blind check measurements of plots used in this report. The columns labeled "Midwestern States" come from all measurements made by FIA crews within the entire 11-state area (North Dakota, South Dakota, Nebraska, Kansas, Minnesota, Iowa, Missouri, Wisconsin, Illinois, Michigan, and Indiana) where the Northern Research Station implemented the FIA program from 2000 through 2004. Training and supervision of crews is a regional effort and crews often work in more than one state. Regional data quality observations reflect the overall measurement quality of all data collected by FIA in the Midwestern States.

In Michigan, many variables such as diameter at breast height have a low tolerance (± 0.1 in.) and a high percentage of data within the tolerance (93.1 percent). Measurements for determining tree-size class are precise. In contrast, a few variables such as stand age have a larger tolerance (± 10 years) and less data within the tolerance (60.4 percent). The estimate of stand age is based on the composition of all age classes within a stand. Often, stands are heterogeneous by age but a single value must be assigned to them. Sometimes this confounds analysis of stand age over time.

In addition to percent compliance to MQOs, the blind check observations were used to test for relative bias in the field-crew measurements. Relative bias is defined here as a tendency for standard field-crew measurements to be higher or lower than measurements taken by the QA crews. The estimated relative bias and limits of 95 percent confidence intervals (based on parametric bootstrap estimates) for the relative bias are presented in Table F.

Blind check measurements do not provide direct observations of true bias in field measurements (average difference between field measurements and true values) because they are paired observations of two field measurements. The QA crew in these blind checks typically has more training and experience with FIA field measurements than the first crew, but both crews use the same methods and instruments to obtain measurements. These methods have been selected to be the best available and for use nationwide by FIA; they are commonly used by similar natural-resource inventories. A basic assumption is that when applied correctly these methods provide unbiased observations of the attribute they are designed to measure. Under this assumption, relative bias observations in Table F provide observations of bias due to the difference in experience and training between the field and QA crews. In most cases, there is no significant bias.

Prediction Error

Errors associated with mathematical models (such as volume models) aimed at providing observations of the attributes of interest based on sample attributes are called prediction errors. Area, number of trees, volume, biomass, growth, removals, and mortality are the primary attributes of interest presented in this report. Estimates of area and number of trees are based on direct observation and do not rely on prediction models. Models are used to predict volume and biomass estimates of individual-tree volumes. Change estimates such as growth, mortality, and removals are based on these model-based predictions of volume from both the current plot measurements and the measurements taken in the previous inventory.

Estimates of prediction errors associated with the volume models in this report were presented by Hahn (1984), along with model forms, methods used in model development, and model-parameter estimates. The estimated prediction errors are based on observations of 101,642 trees measured in the forest inventories of Michigan (1980), Minnesota (1977), and Wisconsin (1968). For gross cubic-foot volume of a live tree, standard errors ranged from 1.47 to 28.13 ft^3. For board-foot volume of a live tree, standard errors ranged from 14.49 to 189.95 board feet.

In comparing FIA estimates to other data sources, users need to be aware of the prediction models used in both estimates. If both estimates are based on the same prediction models with matching fitted parameter values, the prediction bias of one estimate should cancel out that of the other estimate. If the estimates are based on different prediction models, the prediction error of both models must be considered

Nonresponse Error

Nonresponse error occurs when crews are unable to measure a plot (or a portion of a plot) at a selected location. Nonresponse falls into the following three classes:

- Denied access – Entire plots or portions of plots where the field crew is unable to obtain permission from the landowner to measure trees on the plot.
- Hazardous/inaccessible – Entire plots or portions of plots where conditions prevent a crew from safely accessing the plot or measuring trees on the plot.
- Other – Plots where the field crew is unable to obtain a valid measurement for reasons other than those stated.

Nonresponse has two effects on the sample. First, it reduces the sample size. The reduced sample size is reflected in the sampling errors. Second, nonresponse can bias the estimates if the portion of the population not being sampled differs from the portion being sampled.

In FIA, nonresponse rates are relatively low. In the 2004 Michigan inventory, 18,916 sample plots were selected for observation. Almost 98 percent of these are included in the sample used to estimate current resources. On 647 plots, crews were unable to obtain owner permission to measure the plot or part of the plot; hazardous conditions on 15 plots prevented the crew from measuring all or part of the plot.

Even an overall nonresponse rate of 1 percent can cause considerable bias if not properly taken into account. The major source of nonresponse is denied access to plots, which occurs primarily on lands in private ownership. Also, observations for plots on nonforest and water land classes rarely require crews to physically enter the land. Nor is permission needed because the observation can be obtained from aerial photos or other sources of remotely sensed information.

The stratified estimation process used by FIA with strata defined by three ownership classes (national forest, other public, and private) and four Landsat TM forest cover classes (nonforest, nonforest edge, forest edge, and forest) reduces the possible effects of bias caused by nonresponse. Under the stratified estimation process used by FIA, nonresponses are removed from the sample, and stratum estimates (means, totals, and sampling errors) are obtained only from plots with valid observations. The net effect in the estimates of means and totals is that the average of the observed plots within the stratum (ownership-forest-cover class) becomes the estimate for all nonresponses within that stratum. The nonresponse rate in one stratum does not affect the estimate in other strata. The response rate within each stratum is presented in Table G for the Michigan 2004 inventory and for all FIA inventories conducted in the Midwest by the Northern Research Station over the same period.

In Table 1 of this report we acknowledge denied access and hazardous conditions as two land classes in Michigan within which we are unable to provide estimates on variables such as forest area and timber volume. However, we do report the total estimated area in each of these classes. In all other tables of this report, we do not acknowledge either of these classes, and in the estimation process we treat the sample where we do have observations as a random sample of the entire State.

The nonresponse plots in this inventory were not permanently removed from the FIA system of plots. In future inventories we will again attempt to measure these plots. At that time we may be able to obtain permission to access these plots, hazardous conditions may have changed, and other circumstances that caused us to drop plots from a specific inventory cycle may well be different.

GLOSSARY

Average annual mortality: The average annual volume of trees that died (cause of death not due to harvesting or land clearing) during the period between inventories. This estimate can be provided in cubic feet for live and growing-stock trees that died or in board feet for sawtimber trees that died.

Average annual net growth: The average annual change in the volume of trees during the period between inventories. Components include the change in volume of trees that have met the minimum size requirements over the inventory period, plus the volume of trees reaching the minimum size during the period (ingrowth), minus the volume of trees that died during the period, minus the volume of cull during the period. Mortality removals (trees killed due to harvesting and left on site), diversion removals (change from forest land to nonforest land), and reclassifications (change from timberland to reserved or less productive forest land) are not included. This estimate can be provided in cubic feet for live and growing-stock trees or in board feet for sawtimber trees.

Average annual removals: The average annual volume of trees removed from forest or timberland during the period between inventories. The estimate includes harvest removals (cut and utilized), mortality removals (killed due to harvesting and left on site), diversion removals (change from forest land to nonforest land), and reclassifications (change from timberland to reserved or less productive forest land). This estimate can be provided in cubic feet for live and growing-stock trees or in board feet for sawtimber trees.

Basal area: Tree area in square feet of the cross section at breast height of a single tree. When the basal areas of all trees in a stand are summed, the result usually is expressed as square feet of basal area per acre.

Bioindicator species: A tree, woody shrub, or herb species that responds to ambient levels of ozone pollution with distinct visible foliar symptoms that are easy to diagnose.

Biomass: The aboveground volume of live trees (including bark but excluding foliage) reported in dry tons (dry weight). Biomass has four components:

  Bole: Biomass of a tree from 1 foot above the ground to a 4-inch top outside bark or to a point where the central stem breaks into limbs.

  Tops and limbs: Total biomass of a tree from a 1-foot stump minus the bole.

  1-to 5-inch trees: Total aboveground biomass of a tree from 1 to 5 inches in d.b.h.

  Stump: Biomass of a tree 5 inches d.b.h. and larger from the ground to a height of 1 foot.

Bulk density: The mass of soil per unit volume. A measure of the ratio of pore space to solid materials in a given soil. It is expressed in units of grams per cubic centimeter of oven dry soil.

Coarse woody debris (CWD): Dead branches, twigs, and wood splinters 3.0 inches in diameter and larger measured at the smallest end.

Commercial species: Tree species suitable for industrial wood products.

Compacted live crown ratio: The percent of the total length of the tree that supports a full, live crown. To determine compacted live crown ratio for trees that have uneven length crowns, lower branches are visually transferred to fill holes in the upper portions of the crown, until a full, even crown is created.

Corporate: An ownership class of private lands owned by corporations.

County and municipal: An ownership class of public lands owned by counties or local public agencies, or lands leased by these governmental units for more than 50 years. Also known as local government.

Cropland: Land under cultivation within the last 24 months, including cropland harvested, crop failures, cultivated summer fallow, idle cropland used only for pasture, orchards, active Christmas tree plantations indicated by annual shearing, nurseries, and land in soil improvement crops but excluding land cultivated in developing improved pasture.

Crown: The part of a tree or woody plant bearing live branches or foliage.

Crown dieback: Recent mortality of branches with fine twigs, which begins at the terminal portion of a branch and proceeds toward the trunk. Dieback is considered only when it occurs in the upper and outer portions of the tree. When whole branches are dead in the upper crown, without obvious signs of damage such as breaks or animal injury, it is assumed the branches died from the terminal portion of the branch. Dead branches in the lower portion of the live crown are assumed to have died from competition and shading.

Cull tree: A live tree, 5.0 inches in d.b.h. or larger, that is unmerchantable for saw logs now or prospectively because of rot, roughness, or species. (see definitions for rotten and rough trees.)

Decay class: Qualitative assessment of stage of decay (five classes) of coarse woody debris based on visual assessments of color of wood, presence/absence of twigs and branches, texture of rotten portions, and structural integrity.

Diameter class: A classification of trees based on diameter outside bark measured at breast height (4-1/2 feet above ground). D.b.h. is the common abbreviation for "diameter at breast height." With 2-inch diameter classes, the 6-inch class, for example, includes trees 5.0 through 6.9 inches d.b.h. A "diameter at root collar" or d.r.c. measurement is acquired at the root collar for multi-stemmed woodland speices (e.g., Rocky Mountain juniper).

Down woody material (DWM): Woody pieces of trees and shrubs that have been uprooted (no longer supporting growth) or severed from their root system, not self-supporting, and lying on the ground.

Duff: A soil layer dominated by organic material derived from the decomposition of plant and animal litter and deposited on either an organic or a mineral surface. This layer is distinguished from the litter layer in that the original organic material has undergone sufficient decomposition that the source of this material (e.g., individual plant parts) no longer can be identified.

Effective cation exchange capacity (ECEC): The sum of cations that a soil can adsorb in its natural pH. It is expressed in units of centimoles of positive charge per kilogram of soil.

Federal: An ownership class of public lands owned by the U.S. Government.

Fiber products: Products derived from wood and bark residues, such as pulp, composition board products, and wood chips.

Fine materials: Wood residues not suitable for chipping, such as planer shavings and sawdust.

Fine woody debris (FWD): Dead branches, twigs, and wood splinters 0.1 to 2.9 inches in diameter.

Forest land: Land at least 10-percent stocked by trees of any size, including land that formerly had such tree cover and that will be naturally or artificially regenerated. Forest land includes transition zones, such as areas between heavily forested and nonforested lands that are at least 10-percent stocked with trees and forest areas adjacent to urban and builtup lands. Also included are pinyon-juniper and chaparral areas in the West and afforested areas. The minimum area for classification of forest land is 1 acre and 120 feet wide measured stem-to-stem from the outer-most edge. Unimproved roads and trails, streams, and clearings in forest areas are classified as forest if less than 120 feet wide.

Forest type: A classification of forest land based on the species presently forming a plurality of the live-tree stocking. If softwoods predominate (50 percent or more), then the forest type will be one of the softwood types and likewise for hardwoods. For the eastern United States, there are mixed hardwood-pine forest types when the pine and/or redcedar (either eastern or southern) component is between 25 and 49 percent of the stocking. If the pine/redcedar component is less than 25 percent of the stocking, then one of the hardwood forest types is assigned. The following are common or well known forest types in the State of Michigan:

Jack pine: Associates – northern pin oak, bur oak, red pine, bigtooth aspen, paper birch, northern red oak, eastern white pine, red maple, balsam fir, white spruce, black spruce, and tamarack. Sites – dry to mesic sites. Softwood forest type that is a member of the white/red/jack pine forest-type group.

Red pine: Associates – eastern white pine, jack pine, red maple, northern red oak, white spruce, balsam fir, quaking aspen, bigtooth aspen, paper birch, northern pin oak. Sites – common on sandy soils but reaches best development on well drained sandy loam to loam soils. Softwood forest type that is a member of the white/red/jack pine forest-type group.

Eastern white pine/ eastern hemlock (includes Carolina hemlock): Associates – beech, sugar maple, basswood, red maple, yellow birch, gray birch, red spruce, balsam fir, black cherry, white ash, paper birch, sweet birch, northern red oak, white oak, chestnut oak, yellow-poplar, and cucumbertree. Sites – wide variety but favors cool locations, moist ravines, and north slopes. Softwood forest type that is a member of the white/red/jack pine forest-type group.

Eastern white pine: Associates – pitch pine, gray birch, aspen, red maple, pin cherry, white oak, paper birch, sweet birch, yellow birch, black cherry, white ash, northern red oak, sugar maple, basswood, hemlock, northern white-cedar, yellow-poplar, white oak, chestnut oak, scarlet oak, and shortleaf pine. Sites – wide variety but best development on well drained sands and sandy loams. Softwood forest type that is a member of the white/red/jack pine forest-type group.

Eastern hemlock (includes Carolina hemlock): Associates – white pine, balsam fir, red spruce, beech, sugar maple, yellow birch, basswood, red maple, black cherry, white ash, paper birch, sweet birch, northern red oak, and white oak. Sites – cool locations, moist ravines, and north and east slopes. Softwood forest type that is a member of the white/red/jack pine forest-type group.

Balsam fir: Associates – black, white, or red spruce; paper or yellow birch; quaking or bigtooth aspen, beech; red maple; hemlock; tamarack; black ash; or northern white-cedar. Sites – upland sites on low-lying moist flats and in swamps. Softwood forest type that is a member of the spruce/fir forest-type group.

White spruce: Associates – black spruce, paper birch, quaking aspen, red spruce, balsam fir, and balsam poplar. Sites – transcontinental; grows well on calcareous and well drained soils but is found on acidic rocky and sandy sites, and sometimes in fen peat lands along the maritime coast. Softwood forest type that is a member of the spruce/fir forest-type group.

Black spruce: Associates – white spruce, quaking aspen, balsam fir, paper birch, tamarack, northern white-cedar, black ash, and red maple. Sites – wide variety from moderately dry to very wet. Softwood forest type that is a member of the spruce/fir forest-type group.

Tamarack: Associates – black spruce, balsam fir, white spruce, northern white-cedar, and quaking aspen. Sites – found on wetlands and poorly drained sites. Softwood forest type that is a member of the spruce/fir forest-type group.

Northern white-cedar: Associates – balsam fir, tamarack, black spruce, white spruce, red spruce, black ash, and red maple. Sites – mainly occurs in swamps but also in seepage areas, limestone uplands, and old fields. Softwood forest type that is a member of the spruce/fir forest-type group.

Scotch pine: Common plantation species. Softwood forest type that is a member of the nonnative softwood forest-type group.

Eastern white pine/northern red oak/white ash: Associates – red maple, basswood, yellow birch, bigtooth aspen, sugar maple, beech, paper birch, black cherry, hemlock, and sweet birch. Sites – deep, fertile, well drained soil. Mixed hardwood-pine forest type and member of the oak/pine forest-type group.

Other pine/hardwood: A type used for those unnamed pine-hardwood combinations that meet the requirements for oak-pine. These are stands where hardwoods (usually oaks) comprise the plurality of the stocking with at least a 25 to 49 percent pine, eastern redcedar, or southern redcedar component. Mixed hardwood-pine forest type and member of the oak/pine forest-type group.

Post oak/blackjack oak (includes dwarf post oak): Associates – black oak, hickory, southern red oak, white oak, scarlet oak, shingle oak, live oak, shortleaf pine, Virginia pine, blackgum, sourwood, red maple, winged elm, hackberry, chinkapin oak, Shumard oak, dogwood, and eastern redcedar. Sites – dry uplands and ridges. Hardwood forest type and member of the oak/hickory forest-type group.

White oak/red oak/hickory (includes all hickories except water and shellbark hickory): Associates – pin oak, northern pin oak, chinkapin oak, black oak, dwarf chinkapin oak, American elm, scarlet oak, bur oak, white ash, sugar maple, red maple, walnut, basswood, locust, beech, sweetgum, blackgum, yellow-poplar, and dogwood. Sites – wide variety of well drained upland soils. Hardwood forest type and member of the oak/hickory forest-type group.

White oak: Associates – black oak, northern red oak, bur oak, hickory, white ash, yellow-poplar. Sites – scattered patches on upland, loamy soils but on drier sites than white oak/red oak/hickory forest type. Hardwood forest type and member of the oak/hickory forest-type group.

Northern red oak: Associates – black oak, scarlet oak, chestnut oak, and yellow-poplar. Sites – spotty distribution on ridge crests and north slopes in mountains but also found on rolling land, slopes, and benches on loamy soil. Hardwood forest type and member of the oak/hickory forest-type group.

Yellow-poplar/white oak/northern red oak: Associates – black oak, hemlock, blackgum, and hickory. Sites – northern slopes, coves, and moist flats. Hardwood forest type and member of the oak/hickory forest-type group.

Sassafras/persimmon: Associates – elm, eastern redcedar, hickory, ash, sugar maple, yellow-poplar, Texas sophora, and oaks. Sites – abandoned farmlands and old fields. Hardwood forest type and member of the oak/hickory forest-type group.

Chestnut oak/black oak/scarlet oak: Associates – northern and southern red oaks, post oak, white oak, sourwood, shagbark hickory, pignut hickory, yellow-poplar, blackgum, sweetgum, red maple, eastern white pine, pitch pine, Table Mountain pine, shortleaf pine, and Virginia pine. Sites – dry upland sites on thin-soiled rocky outcrops on dry ridges and slopes. Hardwood forest type and member of the oak/hickory forest-type group.

Red maple/oak: Associates – the type is dominated by red maple and some of the wide variety of central hardwood associates include upland oak, hickory, yellow-poplar, black locust, sassafras as well as some central softwoods like Virginia and shortleaf pines. Sites – uplands. Hardwood forest type and member of the oak/hickory forest-type group.

Mixed upland hardwoods: Includes Ohio buckeye, yellow buckeye, Texas buckeye, red buckeye, painted buckeye, American hornbeam, American chestnut, eastern redbud, flowering dogwood, hawthorn spp. (e.g., cockspur hawthorn, downy hawthorn, Washington hawthorn, fleshy hawthorn, and dwarf hawthorn), honeylocust, Kentucky coffeetree, Osage orange, all mulberries, blackgum, sourwood, southern red oak, shingle oak, laurel oak, water oak, live oak, willow oak, black locust, blackbead ebony, anacahuita, and September elm. Associates – any mixture of hardwoods of species typical of the upland central hardwood region, should include at least some oak. Sites – wide variety of upland sites. Hardwood forest type and member of the oak/hickory forest-type group.

Black ash/American elm/red maple (includes slippery and rock elm): Associates – swamp white oak, silver maple, sycamore, pin oak, blackgum, white ash, and cottonwood. Sites – moist to wet areas, swamps, gullies, and poorly drained flats. Hardwood forest type and member of the elm/ash/cottonwood forest-type group.

Cottonwood: Associates – willow, white ash, green ash, and sycamore. Sites –streambanks where bare, moist soil is available. Hardwood forest type and member of the elm/ash/cottonwood forest-type group.

Sugarberry/hackberry/elm/green ash (includes American, winged, cedar, slippery and rock elm): Associates – boxelder, pecan, blackgum, persimmon, honeylocust, red maple, and hackberry. Sites – low ridges and flats in flood plains. Hardwood forest type and member of the elm/ash/cottonwood forest-type group. This type was renamed to green ash/red maple/elm for this report. In Michigan, sugarberry is not part of this type.

Green ash/red maple/elm: See sugarberry/hackberry/elm/green ash. Sugarberry/hackberry/elm/ green ash was renamed to green ash/red maple/elm for this report. In Michigan, sugarberry is not part of this type.

Silver maple/American elm: Silver maple and American elm are the majority species in this type. Associates – chalk maple, sweetgum, pin oak, swamp white oak, eastern cottonwood, sycamore, green ash, and other moist-site hardwoods, according to the region. Sites – primarily on well drained moist sites along river bottoms and floodplains, and beside lakes and larger streams. Hardwood forest type and member of the elm/ash/cottonwood forest-type group.

Red maple/lowland: Red maple comprises a majority of the stocking. Because this type grows on a wide variety of sites over an extensive range, associates are diverse. Associates – yellow-poplar, blackgum, sweetgum, and loblolly pine. Site – generally restricted to very moist to wet sites with poorly drained soils, and on swamp borders. Hardwood forest type and member of the elm/ash/cottonwood forest-type group.

Cottonwood/willow (includes peachleaf, black and Bebb willow): Associates – white ash, green ash, sycamore, American elm, red maple and boxelder. Sites – stream banks where bare, moist soil is available. Hardwood forest type and member of the elm/ash/cottonwood forest-type group.

Sugar maple/beech/yellow birch: Associates – butternut, basswood, red maple, hemlock, northern red oak, white ash, white pine, black cherry, sweet birch, American elm, rock elm, and eastern hophornbeam. Sites – fertile, moist, well drained sites.

Black cherry: Associates – sugar maple, northern red oak, red maple, white ash, basswood, sweet birch butternut, American elm, and hemlock. Sites – fertile, moist, well drained sites. Hardwood forest type and member of the maple/beech/birch forest-type group.

Cherry/ash/yellow-poplar: Associates – sugar maple, American beech, northern red oak, white oak, blackgum, hickory, cucumbertree, and yellow birch. Sites – fertile, moist, well drained sites. Hardwood forest type and member of the oak/hickory forest-type group.

Hard maple/basswood (includes American, Carolina, and white basswood): Associates – black maple, white ash, northern red oak, eastern hophornbeam, American elm, red maple, eastern white pine, eastern hemlock. Sugar maple and basswood occur in different proportions but together comprise the majority of the stocking. Sites – fertile, moist, well drained sites. Hardwood forest type and member of the maple/beech/birch forest-type group.

Elm/ash/locust: Associates – Black locust, silver maple, boxelder, blackbead ebony, American elm, slippery elm, rock elm, red maple, green ash predominate. Found in the Midwest, unknown in the Northeast. Sites – upland. Hardwood forest type and member of the oak/hickory forest-type group.

Red maple/upland: Associates – the type is dominated by red maple and some northern hardwood associates include sugar maple, beech, birch, aspen, as well as some northern softwoods like white pine, red pine, and hemlock; this type is often the result of repeated disturbance or cutting. Sites – uplands. Hardwood forest type and member of the maple/beech/birch forest-type group.

Aspen: Associates – Engelmann spruce, lodgepole pine, ponderosa pine, Douglas-fir, subalpine fir, white fir, white spruce, balsam poplar, and paper birch. Sites – aspen has the capacity to grow on a variety of sites and soils, ranging from shallow stony soils and loamy sands to heavy clays. Hardwood forest type and member of the aspen/birch forest-type group.

Paper birch (includes northern paper birch): Associates – aspen, white spruce, black spruce, and lodgepole pine. Sites – can be found on a range of soils but best developed on well drained sandy loam and silt loam soils. Hardwood forest type and member of the aspen/birch forest-type group.

Balsam poplar: Associates – paper birch, white spruce, black spruce, and tamarack. Sites – occurs on rich floodplains where erosion and folding are active. Hardwood forest type and member of the aspen/birch forest-type group.

Forest-type group: Combinations of forest types that share closely associated species or site requirements and are generally combined for brevity of reporting. See forest type for examples of forest-type group members.

Growing stock: A classification of timber inventory that includes live trees of commercial species meeting specified standards of quality or vigor. Rough and rotten cull trees are excluded. When associated with volume, this includes only trees 5.0 inches d.b.h. and larger.

Hardwood: A dicotyledonous tree, usually broad-leaved and deciduous.

Soft hardwoods: A category of hardwood species with wood generally of low specific gravity (less than 0.5). Notable examples include red maple, paper birch, quaking aspen, and American elm.

Hard hardwoods: A category of hardwood species with wood generally of high specific gravity (greater than 0.5). Notable examples include sugar maple, yellow birch, black walnut, and oaks.

Industrial wood: All commercial roundwood products except fuelwood.

Land area: The area of dry land and land temporarily or partly covered by water, such as marshes, swamps, and river flood plains; streams, sloughs, estuaries, and canals less than 200 feet wide; and lakes, reservoirs, and ponds less than 4.5 acres in area.

Litter: Undecomposed or only partially decomposed organic material that can be readily identified (e.g., plant leaves, twigs).

Live cull: A classification that includes live, cull trees. When associated with volume, it is the net volume in live, cull trees that are 5.0 inches d.b.h. and larger.

Local government: An ownership class of public lands owned by counties or local public agencies, or lands leased by these governmental units for more than 50 years. Also known as county or municipal.

Logging residues: The unused portions of growing-stock and nongrowing-stock trees cut or killed by logging and left in the woods.

Merchantable: Refers to a pulpwood or saw log section that meets pulpwood or saw log specifications, respectively.

National Forest: An ownership class of Federal lands, designated by executive order or statute as National Forests or purchase units, and other lands under the administration of the Forest Service, including experimental areas.

Net volume in cubic feet: The gross volume in cubic feet less deductions for rot, roughness, and poor form. Volume is computed for the central stem from a 1-foot stump to a minimum 4.0-inch top diameter outside bark, or to the point where the central stem breaks into limbs.

Noncommercial species: Tree species of typically small size, poor form, or inferior quality, which normally do not develop into trees suitable for industrial wood products.

Noncorporate private: Nongovernmental conservation and natural resource organizations; unincorporated local parternships, associations, and clubs; and Native American communities.

Nonforest land: Land that has never supported forests and lands formerly forested where use of timber management is precluded by development for other uses. (Note: Includes area used for crops, improved pasture, residential areas, city parks, improved roads of any width and adjoining clearings, powerline clearings of any width, and 1- to 4.5-acre areas of water classified by the Bureau of the Census as land. If intermingled in forest areas, unimproved roads and nonforest strips must be more than 120 feet wide, and clearings, etc., must be more than 1 acre in area to qualify as nonforest land.)

Nonstocked areas: Timberland less than 10-percent stocked with live trees.

Other red oaks: A group of species in the genus Quercus that includes scarlet oak, northern pin oak, southern red oak, bear oak, shingle oak, laurel oak, blackjack oak, water oak, pin oak, willow oak, and black oak.

Other white oaks: A group of species in the genus Quercus that includes overcup oak, chestnut oak, and post oak.

Ownership: The property owned by one ownership unit.

Ownership unit: A classification of ownership encompassing all types of legal entities having an ownership interest in land, regardless of the number of people involved. A unit may be an individual, a combination of persons; a legal entity such as a corporation, partnership, club, or trust, or a public agency. An ownership unit has control of a parcel or group of parcels of land.

Ozone: A regional, gaseous air pollutant produced primarily through sunlight-driven chemical reactions of nitrogen dioxide and hydrocarbons in the atmosphere and causing foliar injury to deciduous trees, conifers, shrubs, and herbaceous species.

Ozone bioindicator site: An open area used for ozone injury evaluations on ozone-sensitive species. The area must meet certain site selection guidelines on size, condition, and plant counts to be used for ozone injury evaluations in FIA.

Physiographic class: A classification of soil and water conditions that affect tree growth on a site. The physiographic classes are as follows:

Xeric: Very dry soils where excessive drainage seriously limits both growth and species occurrence. These sites are usually on upland and upper half slopes.

Xeromesic: Moderately dry soils where excessive drainage limits growth and species occurrence to some extent. These sites are usually on the lower half slopes.

Mesic: Deep, well drained soils. Growth and species occurrence are limited only by climate. These include all cove sites (small sheltered bays) and bottomlands (low land) along intermittent streams.

Hydromesic: Moderately wet soils where insufficient drainage or infrequent flooding limits growth and species occurrence to some extent.

Hydric: Very wet sites where excess water seriously limits both growth and species occurrence.

Poletimber trees: Live trees at least 5.0 inches in d.b.h. but smaller than sawtimber trees.

Primary wood-using mill: A mill that converts roundwood products into other wood products. Common examples are sawmills that convert saw logs into lumber and pulpmills that convert pulpwood into wood pulp.

Productivity class: A classification of forest land in terms of potential annual cubic-foot volume growth per acre at culmination of mean annual increment in fully stocked natural stands.

Pulpwood: Roundwood, whole-tree chips, or wood residues used for the production of wood pulp.

Reserved forest land: Forest land withdrawn from timber utilization through statute, administrative regulation, or designation without regard to productive status.

Residues: Bark and woody materials that are generated in primary wood-using mills when roundwood products are converted to other products. Examples include slabs, edgings, trimmings, miscuts, sawdust, shavings, veneer cores and clippings, and pulp screenings. Includes bark residues and wood residues (both coarse and fine materials) but excludes logging residues.

Rotten tree: A live tree of commercial species that does not contain a saw log now or prospectively primarily because of rot (that is, when rot accounts for more than 50 percent of the total cull volume).

Rough tree: (a) A live tree of commercial species that does not contain a saw log now or prospectively primarily because of roughness (that is, when sound cull due to such factors as poor form, splits, or cracks accounts for more than 50 percent of the total cull volume); or (b) a live tree of noncommercial species.

Roundwood products: Logs, bolts, and other round timber generated from harvesting trees for industrial or consumer use.

Salvable dead tree: A downed or standing dead tree considered currently or potentially merchantable by regional standards.

Saplings: Live trees 1.0 inch through 4.9 inches d.b.h.

Saw log: A log meeting minimum standards of diameter, length, and defect, including logs at least 8 feet long, sound and straight, and with a minimum diameter inside bark of 6 inches for softwoods and 8 inches for hardwoods, or meeting other combinations of size and defect specified by regional standards.

Sawtimber tree: A live tree of commercial species containing at least a 12-foot saw log or two noncontiguous saw logs 8 feet or longer, and meeting regional specifications for freedom from defect. Softwoods must be at least 9.0 inches d.b.h. Hardwoods must be at least 11.0 inches d.b.h.

Sawtimber volume: Net volume of the saw-log portion of live sawtimber in board feet, International 1/4-inch rule (unless specified otherwise), from stump to a minimum 7.0 inches top diameter outside bark (d.o.b.) for softwoods and a minimum 9.0 inches top d.o.b. for hardwoods.

Seedlings: Live trees less than 1.0 inch d.b.h. and at least 1 foot in height.

Select red oaks: A group of species in the genus Quercus that includes cherrybark oak, northern red oak, and Shumard oak.

Select white oaks: A group of species in the genus Quercus that includes white oak, swamp white oak, bur oak, swamp chestnut oak, and chinkapin oak.

Site index: An expression of forest site quality based on the height of a free-growing dominant or codominant tree of a representative species in the forest type at age 50.

Snag: A standing dead tree. In the current inventory, a snag must be 5.0 inches d.b.h./d.r.c. and 4.5 feet tall, and have a lean angle less than 45 degrees from vertical. A snag may be either self-supported by its roots, or supported by another tree or snag.

Softwood: A coniferous tree, usually evergreen, having needles or scale-like leaves.

Soil Order: The broadest category or class of soil based largely on the processes that formed the soil as indicated by the presence or absence of diagnostic horizons or layers. Several dominant soil orders in Michigan are as follows:

Alfisols: Moist mineral soils that form mostly in cool to hot humid areas. These soils usually form under deciduous forests and are usually quite productive. These soils are more weathered than Inceptisols but less than Spodosols.

Entisols: Mineral soils with no horizons or only the beginning of horizons. These soils are basically unaltered from their parent material. Soils of this order vary widely in productivity.

Histisols: Organic soils that form in saturated wet conditions. These can occur in any wet area and can be very productive when drained.

Inceptisols: Soils with few diagnostic features that have formed quickly from the parent material. They form under a wide variety of climates. These soils are more advanced than Entisols but less than other orders. They vary widely in productivity.

Mollisols: Organic soils that form in semiarid to semihumid areas mostly under prairie vegetation. These are some of the most productive soils.

Spodosols: Mineral soils that form in humid climates usually where it is cold and temperate. Most of these soils develop naturally under forests. They are not naturally very fertile but can be productive with fertilizer.

Sound dead: The net volume in salvable dead trees.

Species group: A code assigned to each tree species in order to group them for reporting purposes on presentation tables.

Stand: A group of trees on a minimum of 1 acre of forest land that is stocked by trees of any size.

Stand-size class: A classification of the predominant (based on stocking) diameter class of live trees within the condition. Sawtimber or large diameter trees are at least 11.0 inches diameter for hardwoods and at least 9.0 inches diameter for softwoods. Poletimber or medium diameter trees are at least 5.0 inches diameter and smaller than large diameter trees. Seedling-sapling or small diameter trees are less than 5.0 inches diameter. The classes are as follows:

Nonstocked: Forest land stocked with less than 10 percent of full stocking with live trees. Examples are recently cutover areas or recently reverted agricultural fields.

Seedling-sapling or small diameter: Forest land stocked with at least 10 percent of full stocking with live trees with half or more of such stocking in seedlings or saplings or both.

Poletimber or medium diameter: Forest land stocked with at least 10 percent of full stocking with live trees with half or more of such stocking in poletimber or sawtimber trees or both, and in which the stocking of poletimber exceeds that of sawtimber.

Sawtimber or large diameter: Forest land stocked with at least 10 percent of full stocking with live trees with half or more of such stocking in poletimber or sawtimber trees or both, and in which the stocking of sawtimber is at least equal to that of poletimber.

State: An ownership class of public lands owned by states or lands leased by states for more than 50 years. Also a general reference to one of the political and geographic subdivisions of the United States.

Stocking: The degree of occupancy of land by trees, measured by basal area or number of trees by size and spacing, or both, compared to a stocking standard; that is, the basal area or number of trees, or both, required to fully utilize the growth potential of the land.

Timberland: Forest land that is producing or is capable of producing crops of industrial wood and not withdrawn from timber utilization by statute or administrative regulation. (Note: Areas qualifying as timberland are capable of producing in excess of 20 cubic feet per acre per year of industrial wood in natural stands. Currently inaccessible and inoperable areas are included.)

Timber products output: All timber products cut from roundwood and byproducts of wood manufacturing plants. Roundwood products include logs, bolts, or other round sections cut from growing-stock trees, cull trees, salvable dead trees, trees on nonforest land, noncommercial species, sapling-size trees, and limbwood. Byproducts from primary manufacturing plants include slabs, edging, trimmings, miscuts, sawdust, shavings, veneer cores and clippings, and screenings of pulpmills that are used as pulpwood chips or other products.

Tree: A woody plant usually having one or more erect perennial stems, a stem diameter at breast height of at least 3.0 inches, a more or less definitely formed crown of foliage, and a height of at least 15 feet at maturity.

Tree size class: A classification of trees based on diameter at breast height, including sawtimber trees, poletimber trees, saplings, and seedlings.

Tops: The wood of a tree above the merchantable height (or above the point on the stem 4.0 inches d.o.b. or to the point where the central stem breaks into limbs). It includes the usable material in the uppermost stem.

Urban forest land: Land that would otherwise meet the criteria for timberland but is in an urban-suburban area surrounded by commercial, industrial, or residential development and not likely to be managed for the production of industrial wood products on a continuing basis. Wood removed would be for land clearing, fuelwood, or esthetic purposes. Such forest land may be associated with industrial, commercial, residential subdivision, industrial parks, golf course perimeters, airport buffer strips, and public urban parks that qualify as forest land.

Unreserved forest land: Forest land not withdrawn from harvest by statute or administrative regulation. This includes forest lands that are not capable of producing in excess of 20 cubic feet per acre per year of industrial wood in natural stands.

Veneer log: A roundwood product from which veneer is sliced or sawn and that usually meets certain standards of minimum diameter and length and maximum defect.

Water:

> ***Census water:*** Lakes, reservoirs, ponds, and similar bodies of water 4.5 acres in size and larger; and rivers, streams, canals, etc. more than 200 feet wide.

> ***Noncensus water:*** Lakes, reservoirs, ponds, and similar bodies of water 1.0 acre to 4.5 acres in size. Rivers, streams, canals, etc. 30.0 to 200 feet wide.

Weight: The weight of wood and bark, oven-dry basis (approximately 12 percent moisture content).

LITERATURE CITED

Arner, Stanford L.; Woudenberg, Sharon; Waters, Shirley; Vissage, John; MacLean, Colin; Thompson, Mike; Hansen, Mark. 2003 (revised). **National algorithms for determining stocking class, stand size class, and forest type for Forest Inventory and Analysis plots.** Washington, D.C.: U.S. Department of Agriculture, Forest Service, Forest Inventory and Analysis National Program. 65 p. Available: http://www.fia.fs.fed.us/library/field-guides-methods-proc/.

Bechtold, W.A.; Patterson, P.L., eds. 2005. **The enhanced Forest Inventory and Analysis program— national sampling design and estimation procedures.** Gen. Tech. Rep. SRS-80. Asheville, NC: U.S. Department of Agriculture, Forest Service, Southern Research Station. 85 p.

Brand, G.J.; Nelson, M.D.; Wendt, D.G.; Nimerfro, K.K. 2000. **The hexagon/panel system for selecting FIA plots under an annual inventory.** In: McRoberts, R.E.; Reams, G.A.; Van Deusen, P.C., eds. Proceedings of the first annual Forest Inventory and Analysis symposium. Gen. Tech. Rep. NC-213. St. Paul, MN: U.S. Department of Agriculture, Forest Service, North Central Research Station: 8-13.

Chase, C.D.; Pfeifer, R.E.; Spencer, J.S., Jr. 1970. **The growing timber resource of Michigan, 1966.** Resour. Bull. NC-9. St Paul, MN: U.S. Department of Agriculture, Forest Service, North Central Forest Experiment Station. 62 p.

DellaSala, D.A.; Staus, N.L.; Strittholt, J.R.; Hackman, A.; Iacobelli, A. 2001. **An updated protected areas database for the United States and Canada.** Natural Areas Journal. 21(2): 124-135.

Findell, V.E.; Pfeifer, R.E.; Horn, A.G.; Tubbs, C.H. 1960. **Michigan's forest resources.** Stn. Pap. 82. St. Paul, MN: U.S. Department of Agriculture, Forest Service, Lake States Forest Experiment Station. 46 p.

Hahn, J.T. 1984. **Tree volume and biomass equations for the Lake States.** Res. Pap. NC-250. St. Paul, MN: U.S. Department of Agriculture, Forest Service, North Central Forest Experiment Station. 10 p.

Hansen, Mark H.; Brand, Gary J. 2006. **Michigan's forest resources in 2004.** Resour. Bull. NC-255. St. Paul, MN: U.S. Department of Agriculture, Forest Service, North Central Research Station. 41 p.

Hansen. M.H.; Wendt, D.G. 2000. **Using classified Landsat Thematic Mapper data for stratification in a statewide forest inventory.** In: McRoberts, R.E.; Reams, G.A.; Van Deusen, P.C., eds. Proceedings of the first annual Forest Inventory and Analysis symposium. Gen. Tech. Rep. NC-213. St. Paul, MN: U.S. Department of Agriculture, Forest Service, North Central Research Station: 20-27.

Lake States Forest Experiment Station. 1936. **Forest areas and timber volumes in Michigan.** Econ. Notes 5. St. Paul, MN: U.S. Department of Agriculture, Forest Service, Lakes States Forest Experiment Station. 40 p.

Leatherberry, E.C.; Spencer, J.S. 1996. **Michigan forest statistics, 1993.** Resour. Bull. NC-170. St. Paul, MN: U.S. Department of Agriculture, Forest Service, North Central Forest Experiment Station. 144 p.

McRoberts, R.E. 1999. **Joint annual forest inventory and monitoring system: the North Central perspective.** Journal of Forestry. 97: 21-26.

McRoberts, R.E.; Wendt, D.G.; Nelson, M.D.; Hansen, M.H. 2002. **Using a land cover classification based on satellite imagery to improve the precision of forest inventory area estimates.** Remote Sensing of Environment. 80: 1-9.

McRoberts, R.E. 2005. **The enhanced forest inventory and analysis program.** In: Bechtold, W.A.; Patterson, P. L., eds. The enhanced forest inventory and analysis program–national sampling design and estimation procedures. Gen. Tech. Rep. SRS-80. Asheville, NC: U.S. Department of Agriculture, Forest Service, Southern Research Station: 1-10.

Pugh, Scott A.; Hansen, Mark H.; Pedersen, Lawrence D.; Heym, Douglas C.; Butler, Brett J.; Crocker, Susan J.; Meneguzo, Dacia; Perry, Charles H.; Haugen, David E.; Woodall, Christopher; Jepsen, Ed. 2009. **Michigan's forests 2004.** Resour. Bull. NRS-34. Newtown Square, PA: U.S. Department of Agriculture, Forest Service, Northern Research Station. 210 p.

Raile, G.K.; Smith, W.B. 1983. **Michigan forest statistics, 1980.** Resour. Bull. NC-67. St Paul, MN: U.S. Department of Agriculture, Forest Service, North Central Forest Experiment Station. 101 p.

Schmidt, T.L.; Spencer, J.S.; Bertsch, R. 1997. **Michigan's forests 1993: an analysis.** Resour. Bull. NC-179. St Paul, MN: U.S. Department of Agriculture, Forest Service, North Central Forest Experiment Station. 96 p.

Spencer, J.S. 1983. **Michigan's fourth forest inventory: area.** Resour. Bull. NC-68. St. Paul, MN: U.S. Department of Agriculture, Forest Service, North Central Forest Experiment Station. 39 p.

U.S. Department of Agriculture, Forest Service. 2003. **Forest inventory and analysis national core field guide; Volume I: Field data collection procedures for phase 2 plots. Volume II: Field data collection procedures for phase 3 plots. Version 2.0.** St. Paul, MN: U.S. Department of Agriculture, Forest Service, North Central Research Station. 410 p. Available at http://nrs.fs.fed.us/fia/data-collection (August 4, 2010).

Vogelmann, J.E.; Howard, S.M.; Yang, L.; Larson, C.R.; Wylie, B.K.; Van Driel, N. 2001. **Completion of the 1990s National Land Cover Data Set for the conterminous United States from Landsat Thematic Mapper data and ancillary data sources.** Photogrammetric Engineering and Remote Sensing. 67: 650-662.

Woodall, C. W.; Monleon, V. J. 2008. **Sampling protocol, estimation, and analysis procedures for the down woody materials indicator of the FIA program.** Gen. Tech. Rep. NRS-22. Newtown Square, PA: U.S. Department of Agriculture, Forest Service, Northern Research Station. 68 p.

TABLE TITLES

Tables of Quality Assurance

Table A.—Area and number of plots in each stratum, Michigan, 2004

Table B.—Timberland area by forest type using former and current classification methods, Michigan 1993 and 2004

Table C.—Timberland area by stand-size class using former and current classification methods, Michigan 1993 and 2004

Table D.—State-level estimates of major forest resource attributes and their sampling errors, Michigan, 2004

Table E.—Percent compliance to measurement quality objectives (MQO) tolerances of variables for blind check plots, 2004

Table F.—Observed relative bias values (average [field crew – QA crew]) for measurement variables, blind check plots, 2004

Table G.—FIA nonresponse by strata for selected inventories, 2004

Tables of Estimates

Gaps in the enumeration of tables are placeholders for future reports.

Area

Table 1.—Percentage of area by land status, Michigan, 2004

Table 2.—Area of forest land, in thousand acres, by owner class and forest-land status, Michigan, 2004

Table 3.—Area of forest land, in thousand acres, by forest-type group and productivity class, Michigan, 2004

Table 4.—Area of forest land, in thousand acres, by forest-type group, ownership group, and land status, Michigan, 2004

Table 5.—Area of forest land, in thousand acres, by forest-type group and stand-size class, Michigan, 2004

Table 6.—Area of forest land, in thousand acres, by forest-type group and stand-age class, Michigan, 2004

Table 7.—Area of forest land, in thousand acres, by forest-type group and stand origin, Michigan, 2004

Table 8.—Area of forest land, in thousand acres, by forest-type group and disturbance class, Michigan, 2004

Table 9.—Area of timberland, in thousand acres, by forest-type group and stand-size class, Michigan, 2004

Number

Table 10.—Number of live trees (at least 1 inch d.b.h./d.r.c.), in thousand trees, on forest land by species group and diameter class, Michigan, 2004

Table 11.—Number of growing-stock trees (at least 5 inches d.b.h.), in thousand trees, on timberland by species group and diameter class, Michigan, 2004

Volume

Table 12.—Net volume of live trees (at least 5 inches d.b.h./d.r.c.), in million cubic feet, by owner class and forest-land status, Michigan, 2004

Table 13.—Net volume of live trees (at least 5 inches d.b.h./d.r.c.), in million cubic feet, on forest land by forest-type group and stand-size class, Michigan, 2004

Table 14.—Net volume of live trees (at least 5 inches d.b.h./d.r.c.), in million cubic feet, on forest land by species group and ownership group, Michigan, 2004

Table 15.—Net volume of live trees (at least 5 inches d.b.h./d.r.c.), in million cubic feet, on forest land by species group and diameter class, Michigan, 2004

Table 16.—Net volume of live trees (at least 5 inches d.b.h./d.r.c.), in million cubic feet, on forest land by forest-type group and stand origin, Michigan, 2004

Table 17.—Net volume of growing-stock trees (at least 5 inches d.b.h.), in million cubic feet, on timberland by species group and diameter class, Michigan, 2004

Table 18.—Net volume of growing-stock trees (at least 5 inches d.b.h.), in million cubic feet, on timberland by species group and ownership group, Michigan, 2004

Table 19.—Net volume of sawtimber trees, in million board feet (International ¼-inch rule), on timberland by species group and diameter class, Michigan, 2004

Table 19a.—Net volume of sawtimber trees, in million board feet (Doyle rule), on timberland by species group and diameter class, Michigan, 2004

Table 20.—Net volume of saw-log portion of sawtimber trees, in million cubic feet, on timberland by species group and ownership group, Michigan, 2004

Growth, Mortality, and Removals

Table 24.—Average annual net growth of growing-stock trees (at least 5 inches d.b.h.), in million cubic feet, on timberland by species group and ownership group, Michigan, 1993 to 2004

Table 28.—Average annual mortality of growing-stock trees (at least 5 inches d.b.h.), in million cubic feet, on timberland by species group and ownership group, Michigan, 1993 to 2004

Table 30.—Average annual removals of growing-stock trees (at least 5 inches d.b.h.), in million cubic feet, on timberland by species group and ownership group, Michigan, 1993 to 2004

Weight

Table 31.—Aboveground dry weight of live trees (at least 1 inch d.b.h./d.r.c.), in thousand dry short tons, by owner class and forest-land status, Michigan, 2004

Table 32.—Aboveground dry weight of live trees (at least 1 inch d.b.h./d.r.c.), in thousand dry short tons, on forest land by species group and diameter class, Michigan, 2004

County Level

Table 54.—Area of forest land, in thousand acres, by forest inventory unit, county, and forest-land status, Michigan, 2004

Table 55.—Area of forest land, in thousand acres, by forest inventory unit, county, ownership group, and forest-land status, Michigan, 2004

Table 56.—Area of forest land, in thousand acres, by forest inventory unit, county, and forest-type group, Michigan, 2004

Table 57.—Area of timberland, in thousand acres, by forest inventory unit, county, and stand-size class, Michigan, 2004

Table 58.—Area of timberland, in thousand acres, by forest inventory unit, county, and stocking class, Michigan, 2004

Table 59.—Net volume of growing-stock trees (at least 5 inches d.b.h.), in million cubic feet, and sawtimber trees, in million board feet (International ¼-inch rule), on timberland by forest inventory unit, county, and major species group, Michigan, 2004

Table 59a.—Net volume of growing-stock trees (at least 5 inches d.b.h.), in million cubic feet, and sawtimber trees, in million board feet (Doyle rule), on timberland by forest inventory unit, county, and major species group, Michigan, 2004

Table 60.—Average annual net growth of growing-stock trees (at least 5 inches d.b.h.), in million cubic feet, and sawtimber trees, in million board feet (International ¼-inch rule), on timberland by forest inventory unit, county, and major species group, Michigan, 1993 to 2004

Table 61.—Average annual removals of growing-stock trees (at least 5 inches d.b.h.), in million cubic feet, and sawtimber trees, in million board feet (International ¼-inch rule), on timberland by forest inventory unit, county, and major species group, Michigan, 1993 to 2004

Table 61a.—Average annual removals of growing-stock trees (at least 5 inches d.b.h.), in million cubic feet, and sawtimber trees, in million board feet (Doyle rule), on timberland by forest inventory unit, county, and major species group, Michigan, 1993 to 2004

Table 65.—Sampling errors, in percent, for net volume, average annual net growth, average annual removals, and average annual mortality on timberland, and forest and timberland area by forest inventory unit and county, Michigan, 2004

Table A.—Area and number of plots in each stratum, Michigan, 2004

Unit[a]	Ownership layer[b]	Classified NLCD layer[c]	Area[d]	Selected[e]	Nonforest office plots[f]	Field check plots[g]	Field check plots measured[h]	Forest plots measured[i]	Forest plots measured for change[j]	Plots not measured[k]
			-- acres[d] --				--- number of plots ---			
					Public lands					
1 & 2	Hiawatha NF	Nonforest	12,000	11	5	6	6	5	2	0
		Nonforest edge	55,000	19	3	16	16	16	3	0
		Forest	706,000	324	9	315	315	315	89	0
		Forest edge	123,000	57	5	52	52	52	12	0
		Total	896,000	411	22	389	389	388	106	0
2	Ottawa NF	Nonforest - nonforest edge	38,000	28	6	22	22	21	5	0
		Forest	862,000	411	8	403	403	403	111	0
		Forest edge	87,000	37	2	35	35	35	15	0
		Total	987,000	476	16	460	460	459	131	0
3 & 4	Huron-Manistee NF	Nonforest - nonforest edge	36,000	9	3	6	6	6	2	0
		Forest	833,000	431	3	428	426	425	130	2
		Forest edge	88,000	51	2	49	49	48	19	0
		Total	957,000	491	8	483	481	479	151	2
1	Other public	Nonforest	85,000	49	33	16	16	15	2	0
		Nonforest edge	160,000	86	34	52	52	49	4	0
		Forest	919,000	429	10	419	419	418	65	0
		Forest edge	245,000	135	17	118	117	113	23	1
		Total	1,409,000	699	94	605	604	595	94	1
2	Other public	Nonforest - nonforest edge	65,000	27	3	24	23	22	3	1
		Forest	741,000	370	7	363	363	359	42	0
		Forest edge	111,000	62	2	60	58	55	9	2
		Total	917,000	459	12	447	444	436	54	3
3	Other public	Nonforest	36,000	11	9	2	2	0	0	0
		Nonforest edge	134,000	68	18	50	50	45	8	0
		Forest	1,681,000	832	10	822	821	815	150	1
		Forest edge	310,000	163	13	150	149	143	27	1
		Total	2,161,000	1,074	50	1,024	1,022	1,003	185	2

Continued

33

Table A.—continued

Unit[a]	Ownership layer[b]	Classified NLCD layer[c]	Area	Selected[e]	Nonforest office plots[f]	Field check plots[g]	Field check plots measured[h]	Forest plots measured[i]	Forest plots measured for change[j]	Plots not measured[k]
4	Other public	Nonforest	47,000	21	21	0	0	0	0	0
		Nonforest edge	55,000	38	10	28	27	23	2	1
		Forest	195,000	94	3	91	91	90	19	0
		Forest edge	81,000	38	4	34	34	33	7	0
		Total	378,000	191	38	153	152	146	28	1
Total all public lands			7,705,000	3,801	240	3,561	3,552	3,506	749	9
		Private lands								
1	Private	Nonforest	338,000	169	157	12	12	10	0	0
		Nonforest edge	357,000	175	70	105	105	96	20	0
		Forest	1,663,000	920	9	911	894	890	147	17
		Forest edge	494,000	248	20	228	222	211	47	6
		Total	2,852,000	1,512	256	1,256	1,233	1,207	214	23
2	Private	Nonforest	227,000	105	96	9	9	5	0	0
		Nonforest edge	313,000	186	70	116	108	102	26	8
		Forest	2,749,000	1,417	9	1,408	1,378	1,368	214	30
		Forest edge	495,000	235	26	209	206	191	39	3
		Total	3,784,000	1,943	201	1,742	1,701	1,666	279	41
3	Private	Nonforest	1,828,000	968	911	57	51	25	4	6
		Nonforest edge	1,679,000	824	469	355	328	279	42	27
		Forest	3,234,000	1,646	49	1,597	1,457	1,442	209	140
		Forest edge	1,906,000	961	214	747	663	623	138	84
		Total	8,647,000	4,399	1,643	2,756	2,499	2,369	393	257
4	Private	Nonforest	7,739,000	3,959	3,791	168	145	55	14	23
		Nonforest edge	3,105,000	1,603	928	675	582	433	85	93
		Forest	1,184,000	611	33	578	503	486	102	75
		Forest edge	2,328,000	1,088	257	831	712	633	127	119
		Total	14,356,000	7,261	5,009	2,252	1,942	1,607	328	310
Total all private lands			29,639,000	15,115	7,109	8,006	7,375	6,849	1,214	631
Total all lands			37,344,000	18,916	7,349	11,567	10,927	10,355	1,963	640

Table A—Footnote

[a] The following table lists the counties in each group used to define the estimation strata.

Unit 1	Unit 2	Unit 3		Unit 4	
Alger	Baraga	Alcona	Leelanau	Allegan	Livingston
Chippewa	Dickinson	Alpena	Manistee	Barry	Macomb
Delta	Gogebic	Antrim	Mason	Berrien	Monroe
Luce	Houghton	Arenac	Mecosta	Branch	Montcalm
Mackinac	Iron	Bay	Midland	Calhoun	Muskegon
Menominee	Keweenaw	Benzie	Missaukee	Cass	Oakland
Schoolcraft	Marquette	Charlevoix	Montmorency	Clinton	Ottawa
	Ontonagon	Cheboygan	Newaygo	Eaton	Saginaw
		Clare	Oceana	Genesee	St. Joseph
		Crawford	Ogemaw	Gratiot	Sanilac
		Emmet	Osceola	Hillsdale	Shiawassee
		Gladwin	Oscoda	Huron	Tuscola
		Grand Traverse	Otsego	Ingham	Van Buren
		Iosco	Presque Isle	Ionia	Washtenaw
		Isabella	Roscommon	Jackson	Wayne
		Kalkaska	Wexford	Kalamazoo	
		Lake		Kent	
				Lapeer	

[b] Ownership layer – Classification based on Protected Areas Database.

[c] Classified NLCD layer – Classification based on the 1992 NLCD classification and 2-pixel edge zones.

[d] Area (Acres) – Total area defined by intersection of ownership and classified NLCD layers within group of counties specified.

[e] Selected – Total number of plots selected to be sampled.

[f] Nonforest office plots – Selected plots whose observed classification as nonforest based on examination of aerial photographs and/or digital orthoquads.

[g] Field check plots – Selected plots that required field measurement.

[h] Field check plots measured– Field check plots where measurement was completed successfully. Excludes plots that were denied access, hazardous, or lost and measurement was not possible.

[i] Forest plots measured – Field check plots where forest condition was present on plot and measurement was completed in 2004 inventory. These plots are used to estimate current conditions, e.g., area, volume, number of trees, and biomass.

[j] Forest plots measured for change– Field check plots measured in both 1993 inventory and 2004 inventory where a forest condition was found on plot and measurement was completed. These plots are used to estimate change between inventories, e.g., growth, removals, mortality, and area change.

[k] Plots not measured – Plots selected for field measurement but not measured due to denied access, hazardous condition, or other complications.

Table B.—Timberland area by forest type using former and current classification methods, Michigan 1993 and 2004

Forest type or forest-type group	1993		2004
	Published	Revised	
	- - - - - - - - - - *thousand acres* - - - - - - - - - -		
Softwoods:			
Jack pine	731	795	654
Red pine	897	768	850
Eastern white pine	234	159	252
White pine / hemlock [a]		9	26
Eastern hemlock [a]		145	165
Balsam fir	563	327	376
White spruce	147	91	139
Black spruce	465	393	453
Tamarack	149	158	197
Northern white-cedar	1,349	1,177	1,306
Eastern redcedar [a]		2	3
Scotch pine	115	94	133
Other softwoods types [b]		13	42
Total all softwood types	4,651	4,131	4,596
Hardwoods:			
Oak / pine [a]		549	517
Oak / hickory	1,982	2,741	2,571
Oak / gum / cypress [a]		4	57
Elm / ash / cottonwood	1,627	634	1,447
Maple / beech / birch	7,161	6,859	6,304
Aspen	2,676	2,880	2,527
Paper birch	292	498	317
Balsam poplar	190	271	254
Other exotic hardwoods [a]		0	7
Total all hardwood types	13,927	14,435	13,999
Nonstocked			
Nonstocked	39	50	151
Total all types	18,616	18,616	18,746

[a] New forest type that was not identified in the periodic inventories.

[b] Other softwood types consist of several exotic and western forest types such including blue spruce and Douglas-fir. These are primarily old Christmas tree farms.

Table C.—Timberland area by stand-size class using former and current classification methods, Michigan 1993 and 2004

Stand-size class	1993			2004
	Published	Revised		
	Includes modeled plots	Includes modeled plots	No modeled plots	
	------------------------ thousand acres ------------------------			
Sawtimber	8,605	7,473	5,824	7,504
Poletimber	5,541	8,101	8,444	7,486
Seedling/sapling	4,431	3,014	4,064	3,606

Table D.—State-level estimates of major forest resource attributes and their sampling errors, Michigan, 2004

Item	State total	Sampling error
Growing Stock:	*million cubic feet*	*percent*
Volume	27303.2	0.79
Average annual net growth	923.3	3.36
Average annual removals	291.2	7.05
Average annual mortality	224.5	4.90
Sawtimber:	*million board feet* [a]	
Volume	78891.0	1.07
Average annual net growth	3304.1	3.79
Average annual removals	482.9	7.97
Average annual mortality	489.8	6.80
Area:	*thousand acres*	
Forest land	19311.9	0.37
Timberland	18745.7	0.41
Biomass (aboveground live trees):	*million dry tons*	
Forest land	793.7	0.70
Timberland	769.8	0.72

[a] International ¼-inch rule

Table E.—Percent compliance to measurement quality objectives (MQO) tolerances of variables for blind check plots, 2004

Variable	MQO Tolerance	MQO Objective	Michigan Percentage of data within tolerance	Michigan Number of observations	Midwestern States Percentage of data within tolerance	Midwestern States Number of observations
			Tree level			
Diameter at breast height	± 0.1 /20 in.	95	93.1	8,092	92.7	23,933
Diameter at root collar	± 0.1 /20 in.	95	--	0	60.7	28
Azimuth	± 10 °	90	98.4	8,092	98.4	23,961
Horizontal distance	± 0.2 /1.0 ft	90	96.7	8,092	97.1	23,961
Species	No tolerance	95	95.6	8,092	96.2	23,961
Tree genus	No tolerance	99	99.1	8,086	99.2	23,951
Tree status	No tolerance	95	99.4	8,092	99.1	23,961
Rotten/missing cull	± 10 percent	90	99.0	5,756	98.6	16,444
Total length	± 10 percent	90	81.4	5,516	82.3	15,512
Actual length	± 10 percent	90	80.8	567	79.8	1,745
Compacted crown ratio	± 10 percent	90	84.8	7,422	87.6	21,490
Uncompacted crown ratio	± 10 percent	90	79.8	267	79.4	878
Crown class	No tolerance	85	82.5	7,422	83.1	21,490
Decay class	± 1 class	90	94.7	647	95.0	2,199
Cause of death	No tolerance	80	97.8	647	93.5	2,199
Condition	No tolerance	99	96.8	8,092	97.4	23,961
Crown position	No tolerance		77.0	209	80.8	714
Crown light exposure	± 1 class	85	90.3	267	91.0	878
Sapling crown-vigor class	No tolerance	85	81.0	58	66.1	165
Crown density	± 10 percent	90	76.6	209	70.3	714
Crown dieback	± 10 percent	90	96.2	209	96.8	714
Transparency	± 10 percent	90	85.2	209	85.7	714
NC tree class	No tolerance	90	93.9	8,049	92.4	23,610
NC damage agent 1	No tolerance	90	92.0	7,422	92.0	21,490
NC damage agent 2	No tolerance	90	87.3	1,155	87.0	3,420
Utilization	No tolerance	99	--	0	88.7	326
North Central (NC) tree grade	No tolerance	90	74.5	47	68.2	3,826
D.b.h. of live and sound dead trees	± 0.1 /20 inch	95	69.5	1,404	92.5	21,972
D.b.h. of dead rotten trees	± 1 /20 inch	95	92.9	7,580	98.5	997
Total length trees 40 ft plus	± 10 percent	90	98.6	359	83.7	12,763
Total length trees < 40 ft	± 10 percent	90	82.2	4,598	76.1	2,749
Total length trees < 5 inches d.b.h.	± 10 percent	90	77.3	918	71.7	180
			Seedling level			
Species	No tolerance	85	92.2	1,613	91.3	5,031
Genus	No tolerance	90	97.7	1,613	97.2	5,031
Seedling count	± 20 percent	90	60.8	1,613	66.6	5,031
Seedling count coded	No tolerance	90	69.8	1,613	73.2	5,031
			Condition level			
Condition status	No tolerance	99	98.5	647	99.1	2,011
Reserve status	No tolerance	99	99.4	647	99.4	2,011
Owner group	No tolerance	99	98.3	520	98.4	1,598

Continued

Table E.—continued

Variable	MQO		Michigan		Midwestern States	
	Tolerance	Objective	Percentage of data within tolerance	Number of observations	Percentage of data within tolerance	Number of observations
Forest type (type)	No tolerance	95	78.7	520	80.9	1,598
Forest type (group)	No tolerance	99	89.4	520	89.9	1,598
Stand size	No tolerance	99	85.8	520	87.9	1,598
Regeneration status	No tolerance	99	98.5	520	99.1	1,598
Tree density	No tolerance	99	97.9	520	93.6	1,598
Owner class	No tolerance	99	95.6	520	95.7	1,598
Owner status	No tolerance	99	98.3	520	98.9	1,598
Regeneration species	No tolerance	99	98.3	520	98.9	1,598
Disturbance 1	No tolerance	99	96.5	515	93.1	1,586
Disturbance year 1	± 1 yr	99	40.0	5	80.3	66
Disturbance 2	No tolerance	99	90.5	21	94.5	163
Disturbance year 2	± 1 yr	99	--	0	50.0	4
Disturbance 3	No tolerance	99	100.0	2	91.7	12
Disturbance year 3	± 1 yr	99	--	0	--	0
Treatment 1	No tolerance	99	95.3	515	94.8	1,586
Treatment year 1	± 1 yr	99	92.0	25	91.7	96
Treatment 2	No tolerance	99	95.9	49	87.1	178
Treatment year 2	± 1 yr	99	100.0	1	100.0	13
Treatment 3	No tolerance	99	66.7	3	97.1	35
Treatment year 3	± 1 yr	99	--	0	100.0	5
Physiographic class	No tolerance	80	71.3	520	75.9	1,598
Present nonforest use	No tolerance	90	100.0	243	99.9	758
NC land use	No tolerance	99	93.8	647	93.2	2,011
Subplot level						
Subplot center condition	No tolerance	99	97.0	1,923	97.1	5,507
Microplot center condition	No tolerance	99	96.8	1,923	96.8	5,507
Slope	± 10 percent	90	97.7	1,923	97.5	5,507
Aspect	± 10 °	90	89.4	1,748	88.0	5,082
Snow/Water depth	± 0.5 ft		61.6	1,923	66.8	5,507
Plot level						
Distance to road	No tolerance	90	72.2	493	80.4	1,400
Water on plot	No tolerance	90	85.8	493	87.4	1,400
Road type code	No tolerance	90	67.9	346	76.0	1,028
Recreational use restrictions	No tolerance	90	87.9	346	90.4	1,028
Recreational use 1	No tolerance	90	94.2	346	94.3	1,028
Recreational use 2	No tolerance	90	100.0	2	100.0	16
Recreational use 3	No tolerance	90	--	0	90.9	11
Road access	No tolerance	90	94.1	493	93.9	1,400
Elevation	± 50 ft		83.8	402	82.0	1,258
Latitude (decimal degrees)	± 0.0001 dg	99	91.8	402	91.6	1,268
Longitude (decimal degrees)	± 0.0001 dg	99	91.3	402	90.8	1,268

Continued

Table E.—continued

Variable	MQO		Michigan		Midwestern States	
	Tolerance	Objective	Percentage of data within tolerance	Number of observations	Percentage of data within tolerance	Number of observations
Latitude (ft)	± 140 ft		98.3	402	98.3	1,268
Longitude (ft)	± 140 ft		97.5	402	97.6	1,268
Boundary level						
Boundary change	No tolerance	99	100.0	117	95.3	301
Contrasting condition	No tolerance	99	91.5	117	93.0	301
Left azimuth	± 10 degrees	90	83.8	117	85.0	301
Corner mapped	No tolerance	90	98.3	117	97.3	301
Corner azimuth	±10 degrees	90	75.0	4	63.6	11
Corner distance	±1 ft	90	25.0	4	54.5	11
Right azimuth	±10 degrees	90	86.3	117	85.0	301
Site-index tree level						
Condition list	No tolerance	99	91.8	942	90.9	2,811
Diameter	± 0.1 /20 in.	95	90.6	767	90.2	2,203
Species	No tolerance	95	97.6	942	95.9	2,811
Genus	No tolerance	99	99.9	942	99.7	2,811
Azimuth	± 10 degrees	90	98.4	767	98.1	2,203
Distance	± 5 feet	90	99.9	767	99.5	2,203
Total length	± 10 percent	90	89.6	767	90.8	2,203
Diameter age	± 5 years	95	73.1	767	78.2	2,203
Site-index method	No tolerance	99	99.9	942	99.9	2,811
Field site index	No tolerance	99	96.9	942	93.6	2,811

Table F.—Observed relative bias values (average [field crew – QA crew]) for measurement variables, blind check plots, 2004

Variable	Unit of measure	Michigan				Midwestern States			
		Relative bias	95% Confidence interval Lower limit	Upper limit	Number of observations	Relative bias	95% Confidence interval Lower limit	Upper limit	Number of observations
		Tree level							
Diameter at breast height	inches	-0.05	-0.07	-0.03	4,936	-0.01	-0.02	0.00	23,933
Diameter at root collar	inches	0.00	0.00	0.00		0.11	-0.12	0.43	28
Azimuth	degrees	0.06	-0.21	0.31	4,936	0.29	0.18	0.39	23,961
Horizontal distance	feet	0.01	-0.01	0.04	4,936	0.00	-0.01	0.01	23,961
Species	code	-0.78	-1.79	-0.03	4,936	0.07	-0.29	0.44	23,961
Tree genus	code	-0.75	-1.76	-0.01	4,936	0.08	-0.38	0.47	23,951
Tree status	code	-0.01	-0.02	0.00	4,936	0.00	0.00	0.00	23,961
Rotten/missing cull	%	-0.07	-0.29	0.16	2,929	0.03	-0.03	0.11	16,444
Total length	feet	-0.27	-1.12	0.47	2,676	0.24	-0.05	0.45	15,512
Actual length	feet	-0.69	-4.51	2.01	397	-1.82	-3.61	-0.41	1,745
Compacted crown ratio	%	0.23	-0.02	0.49	4,193	0.41	0.27	0.53	21,490
Uncompacted crown ratio	%	-0.94	-3.07	1.06	101	-5.86	-7.27	-4.57	878
Crown class	code	0.01	-0.01	0.03	4,193	0.02	0.01	0.02	21,490
Decay class	code	0.12	0.06	0.17	594	0.06	0.03	0.08	2,199
Cause of death	code	2.93	1.78	4.34	594	1.44	0.88	2.02	2,199
Condition	code	-0.01	-0.01	-0.01	4,936	0.00	0.00	0.01	23,961
Crown position	code	0.05	-0.02	0.13	79	-0.23	-0.28	-0.18	714
Crown light exposure	code	-0.22	-0.35	-0.09	101	-0.18	-0.24	-0.11	878
Sapling crown-vigor class	code	-0.36	-0.61	-0.09	22	-0.21	-0.30	-0.13	165
Crown density	%	-9.49	-11.96	-6.96	79	-5.47	-6.89	-4.19	714
Crown dieback	%	2.15	1.33	3.07	79	-0.37	-0.89	0.16	714
Transparency	%	2.28	0.73	3.89	79	-3.69	-4.50	-2.86	714
NC tree class	code	0.22	0.10	0.33	4,778	0.10	0.05	0.15	23,610
NC damage agent 1	code	2.22	-1.37	5.83	4,193	5.24	4.14	6.36	21,490
NC damage agent 2	code	-0.31	-14.02	14.06	613	5.80	2.22	9.74	3,420
Utilization	code	-0.04	-0.08	-0.02	163	-0.02	-0.06	0.03	326
NC tree grade	code	5.51	-4.16	14.35	626	0.26	-3.07	4.43	3,826
D.b.h. of live and sound dead trees	inches	-0.06	-0.09	-0.03	4,280	-0.02	-0.03	-0.01	21,972
D.b.h. of dead rotten trees	inches	-0.02	-0.08	0.04	257	-0.04	-0.06	-0.01	997
Total length trees 40 ft plus	feet	1.34	0.98	1.72	2,225	0.84	0.69	1.00	12,763

Continued

Table F.—continued

Variable	Unit of measure	Michigan				Midwestern States			
		Relative bias	95% Confidence interval		Number of observations	Relative bias	95% Confidence interval		Number of observations
			Lower limit	Upper limit			Lower limit	Upper limit	
Total length trees < 40 ft	feet	-8.22	-13.14	-4.12	451	-2.54	-4.04	-1.49	2,749
Total length trees < 5 inches d.b.h.	feet	-1.93	-9.62	4.03	23	2.77	0.70	4.88	180
			Seedling level						
Species	code	0.00	-0.01	0.02	1,613	0.00	-0.01	0.01	5,031
Genus	code	0.00	-0.01	0.01	1,613	0.00	0.00	0.01	5,031
Seedling count	percent	-8.50	-14.80	-4.00	1,613	-10.90	-13.50	-8.40	5,031
Seedling count coded	percent	0.11	0.06	0.17	1,613	0.04	0.02	0.07	5,031
			Condition level						
Condition status	code	0.02	-0.01	0.05	647	0.00	-0.02	0.01	2,011
Reserve status	code	0.00	0.00	0.01	647	0.00	0.00	0.01	2,011
Owner group	code	-0.04	-0.37	0.28	520	-0.04	-0.20	0.10	1,598
Forest type (type)	code	23.49	10.50	38.02	520	14.58	8.89	19.97	1,598
Forest type (group)	code	24.23	11.35	38.94	520	14.58	8.85	19.90	1,598
Stand size	code	-0.03	-0.07	0.01	520	-0.01	-0.03	0.01	1,598
Regeneration status	code	0.00	-0.02	0.01	520	0.00	0.00	0.01	1,598
Tree density	code	0.01	0.00	0.02	520	0.00	-0.01	0.01	1,598
Owner class	code	-0.03	-0.42	0.34	520	-0.05	-0.22	0.12	1,598
Owner status	code	0.01	-0.02	0.05	520	0.00	-0.01	0.02	1,598
Regeneration species	code	-0.49	-2.15	0.72	520	0.10	-0.46	0.62	1,598
Stand age	years	-2.24	-3.13	-1.41	520	-0.72	-1.32	-0.11	1,598
Disturbance 1	code	-0.64	-1.48	0.26	515	-1.65	-2.33	-0.90	1,586
Disturbance year 1	year	1,598.00	-4,800.00	6,397.00	5	1,333.00	485.00	2,181.00	66
Disturbance 2	code	-4.33	-12.02	0.00	21	-1.50	-3.02	-0.12	163
Disturbance year 2	year	0.00	0.00	0.00	0	2,000.00	0.00	5,998.00	4
Disturbance 3	code	0.00	0.00	0.00	2	-6.67	-20.00	0.00	12
Disturbance year 3	year	0.00	0.00	0.00	0	0.00	0.00	0.00	0
Treatment 1	code	0.23	0.06	0.42	515	0.13	-0.03	0.28	1,586
Treatment year 1	year	0.32	0.04	0.62	25	0.11	-0.07	0.30	96
Treatment 2	code	0.00	-1.84	1.84	49	3.71	1.88	5.84	178
Treatment year 2	year	1.00	1.00	1.00	1	0.08	-0.23	0.35	13
Treatment 3	code	-13.30	-40.00	0.00	3	-1.10	-3.40	0.00	35

Continued

43

Table F.—continued

Variable	Unit of measure	Michigan Relative bias	Michigan 95% Confidence interval Lower limit	Michigan 95% Confidence interval Upper limit	Michigan Number of observations	Midwestern States Relative bias	Midwestern States 95% Confidence interval Lower limit	Midwestern States 95% Confidence interval Upper limit	Midwestern States Number of observations
Treatment year 3	year	0.00	0.00	0.00	.	0.00	0.00	0.00	5
Physiographic class	code	0.20	-0.19	0.69	520	0.05	-0.14	0.25	1,598
Present nonforest use	code	0.00	0.00	0.00	243	0.05	0.00	0.16	758
NC land use	code	0.20	-0.34	0.78	647	0.03	-0.24	0.26	2,011
Subplot level									
Subplot center condition	code	0.00	-0.01	0.01	1,923	0.00	0.00	0.01	5,507
Microplot center condition	code	0.00	-0.01	0.01	1,923	0.00	0.00	0.01	5,507
Slope	%	1.85	-1.08	4.53	1,923	0.69	-0.34	1.78	5,507
Aspect	degrees	-0.21	-3.27	2.96	1,748	0.09	-1.54	1.53	5,082
Snow/water depth	feet	0.08	-0.15	0.31	1,923	-0.44	-0.84	-0.16	5,507
Plot level									
Distance to Road	code	-0.03	-0.13	0.06	493	0.00	-0.05	0.04	1,400
Water on Plot	code	0.04	-0.18	0.24	493	0.12	0.01	0.21	1,400
Road type code	code	0.01	-0.10	0.11	346	0.07	0.01	0.13	1,028
Recreational use restrictions	code	-0.06	-0.68	0.31	346	0.14	-0.11	0.39	1,028
Recreational use 1	code	-0.03	-0.12	0.05	346	-0.09	-0.15	-0.04	1,028
Recreational use 2	code	0.00	0.00	0.00	2	0.00	0.00	0.00	16
Recreational use 3	code	0.00	0.00	0.00	0	-0.09	-0.36	0.00	11
Road access	code	-0.05	-0.11	-0.01	493	-0.04	-0.07	-0.02	1,400
Elevation	feet	-23.60	-64.80	2.20	402	-34.23	-74.26	-6.51	1,258
Latitude	decimal degrees	0.00	0.00	0.00	402	-0.01	-0.02	0.00	1,268
Longitude	decimal degrees	0.00	0.00	0.00	402	0.66	0.00	1.99	1,268
Latitude	feet	8.50	-10.00	29.30	402	-2,543.00	-6,439.00	-47.50	1,268
Longitude	feet	75.77	-72.38	311.14	402	10,807.00	172.00	30,354.00	1,268
Boundary level									
Boundary change	code	0.00	0.00	0.00	117	0.07	0.03	0.12	301
Contrasting condition	code	0.00	-0.06	0.05	117	0.00	-0.03	0.04	301
Left azimuth	degrees	-7.62	-14.27	-1.70	117	-4.43	-11.22	0.84	301
Corner mapped	code	0.02	0.00	0.04	117	-0.01	-0.03	0.01	301
Corner azimuth	degrees	5.25	-3.00	17.75	4	1.00	-5.05	7.86	11

Continued

44

Table F.—continued

Variable	Unit of measure	Michigan				Midwestern States			
		Relative bias	95% Confidence interval		Number of observations	Relative bias	95% Confidence interval		Number of observations
			Lower limit	Upper limit			Lower limit	Upper limit	
Corner distance	feet	-5.50	-23.50	6.50	4	-1.55	-8.50	2.59	11
Right azimuth	degrees	7.93	2.30	15.16	117	2.19	-2.44	7.10	301
		Site-index tree level							
Condition list	code	-0.18	-0.95	0.39	942	0.21	-0.06	0.41	2,811
Diameter	inches	-0.01	-0.04	0.02	767	-0.01	-0.03	0.01	2,203
Species	code	0.08	-0.12	0.37	942	-0.04	-0.25	0.17	2,811
Genus	code	0.13	0.00	0.38	942	-0.03	-0.24	0.18	2,811
Azimuth	degrees	-0.19	-0.67	0.34	767	-0.11	-0.53	0.34	2,203
Distance	feet	0.03	-0.01	0.06	767	0.04	0.00	0.08	2,203
Total length	feet	-0.10	-0.52	0.32	767	0.22	-0.04	0.49	2,203
Diameter age	years	0.09	-0.39	0.60	767	0.13	-0.14	0.42	2,203
Site-index method	code	0.00	0.00	0.00	942	0.00	0.00	0.00	2,811
Field site index	feet	-0.1	-0.17	-0.02	942	0.45	0.24	0.68	2,811

Table G.—FIA nonresponse by strata for selected inventories, 2004

Owner and strata	Number of plots selected	Observed	Denied access	Hazardous	Other	Percent response rate
	- *number of plots* -					
			Michigan			
National Forest:						
Nonforest	15	15.0	0.0	0.0	0.0	100.0
Nonforest edge	52	52.0	0.0	0.0	0.0	100.0
Forest edge	1,166	1,164.0	2.0	0.0	0.0	99.8
Forest	145	145.0	0.0	0.0	0.0	100.0
Total	1,378	1,376.0	2.0	0.0	0.0	99.9
Other Public:						
Nonforest	85	85.0	0.0	0.0	0.0	100.0
Nonforest edge	215	213.0	1.0	1.0	0.0	99.1
Forest edge	1,725	1,721.8	1.0	2.3	0.0	99.8
Forest	398	394.0	1.0	3.0	0.0	99.0
Total	2,423	2,413.8	3.0	6.3	0.0	99.6
Private:						
Nonforest	5,201	5,170.0	31.0	0.0	0.0	99.4
Nonforest edge	2,788	2,656.5	129.5	2.0	0.0	95.3
Forest edge	4,594	4,327.2	264.5	2.3	0.0	94.2
Forest	2,532	2,313.8	215.9	2.3	0.0	91.4
Total	15,115	14,467.5	640.9	6.5	0.0	95.7
Total	18,916	18,257.3	645.9	12.8	0.0	96.5
			Midwestern States			
National Forest:						
Nonforest	147	147.0	0.0	0.0	0.0	100.0
Nonforest edge	190	189.0	0.0	0.0	1.0	99.5
Forest edge	3,080	3,037.5	5.3	33.3	4.0	98.6
Forest	386	379.0	0.0	5.0	2.0	98.2
Total	3,803	3,752.5	5.3	38.3	7.0	98.7
Other Public:						
Nonforest	1,271	1,268.0	2.0	1.0	0.0	99.8
Nonforest edge	800	795.0	2.0	3.0	0.0	99.4
Forest edge	4,399	4,350.8	10.0	32.3	6.0	98.9
Forest	1,118	1,103.5	4.0	10.5	0.0	98.7
Total	7,588	7,517.3	18.0	46.8	6.0	99.1
Private:						
Nonforest	56,599	56,477.2	119.0	2.8	0.0	99.8
Nonforest edge	12,030	11,610.9	409.2	9.9	0.0	96.5
Forest edge	12,089	11,305.4	759.9	23.7	0.0	93.5
Forest	9,254	8,590.2	651.2	12.7	0.0	92.8
Total	89,972	87,983.7	1,939.3	49.0	0.0	97.8
Total	101,363	99,253.4	1,962.5	134.0	13.0	97.9

Table 1.—Percentage of area by land status, Michigan, 2004

Land status	Percentage of area
Accessible forest land	
Unreserved forest land	
Timberland	48.1
Unproductive	0.6
Total unreserved forest land	48.8
Reserved forest land	
Productive	0.9
Unproductive	0.0
Total reserved forest land	0.9
All accessible forest land	49.6
Nonforest and other land	
Water	
Nonforest land	43.8
Census	2.5
Non-Census	0.6
All nonforest and other land	46.9
Nonsampled land	
Access denied	3.4
Hazardous conditions	0.1
Other	--
All land	100.0
Total area (thousands of acres)	37,344

All table cells without observations in the inventory sample are indicated by --. Table value of 0.0 indicates the percentage rounds to less than 0.1 percent. Columns and rows may not add to their totals due to rounding.

Table 2.—Area of forest land, in thousand acres, by owner class and forest-land status, Michigan, 2004

Owner class	Unreserved forests			Reserved forests			All forest land
	Timberland	Unproductive	Total	Productive	Unproductive	Total	
Forest Service							
National forest	2 505.7	52.2	2 557.9	77.6	0.7	78.3	2 636.2
Other national forest	6.0	--	6.0	--	--	--	6.0
Other Federal							
National Park Service	49.9	3.7	53.6	140.7	3.8	144.5	198.1
Fish and Wildlife Service	31.9	2.1	34.1	1.9	--	1.9	35.9
Department of Defense or Energy	12.4	--	12.4	--	--	--	12.4
Other Federal	27.0	--	27.0	--	--	--	27.0
State and local government							
State	4 026.7	63.6	4 090.3	81.6	--	81.6	4 172.0
Local (county municipal etc)	306.7	2.8	309.5	7.2	--	7.2	316.7
Other non-Federal lands	15.1	--	15.1	--	--	--	15.1
Private							
Undifferentiated private	11 764.3	114.2	11 878.4	12.3	1.8	14.1	11 892.6
All owners	18 745.7	238.6	18 984.2	321.3	6.4	327.7	19 311.9

All table cells without observations in the inventory sample are indicated by -- Table value of 0 0 indicates the acres round to less than 0 1 thousand acres Columns and rows may not add to their totals due to rounding

Table 3.—Area of forest land, in thousand acres, by forest-type group and productivity class, Michigan, 2004

Forest type group	Site productivity class (cubic feet/acre/year)							All classes
	0-19	20-49	50-84	85-119	120-164	165-224	225+	
White / red / jack pine group	71 5	794 0	561 6	470 9	149 0	6 9	2 0	2 055 8
Spruce / fir group	53 1	1 778 8	541 0	175 7	32 0	--	--	2 580 7
Pinyon / juniper group	--	3 3	--	--	--	--	--	3 3
Douglas-fir group	--	--	2 1	2 5	--	--	--	4 5
Fir / spruce / mountain hemlock grou	--	1 9	5 9	5 7	--	--	--	13 6
Exotic softwoods group	2 1	35 5	49 1	42 1	29 5	0 6	--	158 9
Oak / pine group	21 6	176 4	198 8	106 1	36 9	--	--	539 9
Oak / hickory group	12 8	536 9	1 189 4	742 2	85 4	22 7	1 6	2 591 1
Oak / gum / cypress group	--	20 9	11 5	20 1	4 2	--	--	56 6
Elm / ash / cottonwood group	24 2	542 9	480 1	338 2	84 7	2 4	--	1 472 5
Maple / beech / birch group	20 3	2 795 4	2 452 9	1 010 2	167 2	16 5	--	6 462 5
Aspen / birch group	36 0	789 2	1 345 7	911 8	105 3	17 5	4 0	3 209 6
Exotic hardwoods group	3 3	--	2 4	4 5	--	--	--	6 9
Nonstocked	3 3	73 2	46 8	27 6	3 4	1 7	--	156 1
All forest type groups	245 0	7 548 5	6 887 3	3 857 5	697 6	68 4	7 7	19 311 9

All table cells without observations in the inventory sample are indicated by -- Table value of 0 0 indicates the acres round to less than 0 1 thousand acres Columns and rows may not add to their totals due to rounding

Table 4.—Area of forest land, in thousand acres, by forest-type group, ownership group, and land status, Michigan, 2004

Forest type group	Forest Service		Other Federal		State and local government		Undifferentiated private		All forest land
	Timber-land	Other forest land	Timber-land	Other forest land	Timber-land	Other forest land	Timber-land	Other forest land	
White / red / jack pine group	573 7	30 7	22 1	13 2	638 2	47 1	712 5	18 1	2 055 8
Spruce / fir group	357 4	23 3	15 9	38 9	765 5	16 2	1 332 5	30 8	2 580 7
Pinyon / juniper group	- -	- -	- -	- -	- -	- -	3 3	- -	3 3
Douglas-fir group	- -	- -	- -	- -	2 1	- -	2 5	- -	4 5
Fir / spruce / mountain hemlock group	- -	- -	- -	- -	- -	- -	13 6	- -	13 6
Exotic softwoods group	1 7	- -	- -	- -	5 1	- -	150 0	2 1	158 9
Oak / pine group	90 9	11 4	1 8	- -	159 2	5 8	264 8	6 0	539 9
Oak / hickory group	220 6	5 7	13 4	- -	569 5	8 6	1 767 1	6 3	2 591 1
Oak / gum / cypress group	- -	- -	- -	- -	12 6	- -	44 1	- -	56 6
Elm / ash / cottonwood group	77 8	3 8	5 9	- -	273 4	5 1	1 089 5	17 0	1 472 5
Maple / beech / birch group	769 8	41 1	42 0	43 0	1 015 0	52 6	4 476 7	22 3	6 462 5
Aspen / birch group	405 5	12 3	19 3	56 5	868 4	17 3	1 804 6	25 8	3 209 6
Exotic hardwoods group	- -	- -	- -	- -	2 1	- -	4 8	- -	6 9
Nonstocked	14 2	2 2	0 8	0 5	37 5	2 5	98 3	- -	156 1
All forest type groups	2 511 6	130 5	121 3	152 2	4 348 5	155 2	11 764 3	128 3	19 311 9

All table cells without observations in the inventory sample are indicated by -- Table value of 0 0 indicates the acres round to less than 0 1 thousand acres Columns and rows may not add to their totals due to rounding

50

Table 5.—Area of forest land, in thousand acres, by forest-type group and stand-size class, Michigan, 2004

Forest type group	Stand-size class					All size classes
	Large diameter	Medium diameter	Small diameter	Chaparral	Nonstocked	
White / red / jack pine group	1 046.3	695.7	313.7	--	--	2 055.8
Spruce / fir group	660.9	1 219.5	700.3	--	--	2 580.7
Pinyon / juniper group	--	1.1	2.1	--	--	3.3
Douglas-fir group	2.1	2.5	--	--	--	4.5
Fir / spruce / mountain hemlock grou	1.1	2.5	10.0	--	--	13.6
Exotic softwoods group	52.3	65.6	41.1	--	--	158.9
Oak / pine group	193.9	191.7	154.2	--	--	539.9
Oak / hickory group	1 499.5	718.3	373.3	--	--	2 591.1
Oak / gum / cypress group	25.3	23.9	7.4	--	--	56.6
Elm / ash / cottonwood group	545.7	585.8	341.1	--	--	1 472.5
Maple / beech / birch group	3 124.0	2 687.9	650.6	--	--	6 462.5
Aspen / birch group	623.5	1 426.8	1 159.4	--	--	3 209.6
Exotic hardwoods group	2.1	2.4	2.4	--	--	6.9
Nonstocked	--	--	0.5	--	155.6	156.1
All forest type groups	7 776.5	7 623.7	3 756.2	--	155.6	19 311.9

All table cells without observations in the inventory sample are indicated by -- Table value of 0.0 indicates the acres round to less than 0.1 thousand acres Columns and rows may not add to their totals due to rounding

51

Table 6.—Area of forest land, in thousand acres, by forest-type group and stand-age class, Michigan, 2004

Forest type group	Non stocked	Stand-age class (years)											All classes
		1-20	21-40	41-60	61-80	81-100	101-120	121-140	141-160	161-180	181-200	201+	
White / red / jack pine group	--	242 1	514 6	769 6	350 0	102 6	31 7	22 4	11 1	4 2	6 6	--	2 055 8
Spruce / fir group	--	105 0	278 9	701 8	870 8	439 9	113 2	41 8	21 3	2 8	5 3	--	2 580 7
Pinyon / juniper group	--	--	3 3	--	--	--	--	--	--	--	--	--	3 3
Douglas-fir group	--	--	3 7	0 9	--	--	--	--	--	--	--	--	4 5
Fir / spruce / mountain hemlock group	--	8 1	4 4	1 1	--	--	--	--	--	--	--	--	13 6
Exotic softwoods group	--	30 0	78 1	48 5	2 4	--	--	--	--	--	--	--	158 9
Oak / pine group	--	84 4	115 9	188 2	105 7	42 5	2 1	1 2	--	--	--	--	539 9
Oak / hickory group	--	125 2	462 4	792 5	698 6	419 4	72 1	17 3	2 2	--	--	--	2 591 1
Oak / gum / cypress group	--	2 2	13 8	23 6	10 7	6 3	--	--	--	--	--	--	56 6
Elm / ash / cottonwood group	--	67 8	306 3	626 0	341 7	96 7	22 9	5 6	4 1	--	--	--	1 472 5
Maple / beech / birch group	--	285 4	570 0	2 049 7	2 635 6	758 7	99 3	30 4	15 4	3 5	8 0	--	6 462 5
Aspen / birch group	--	617 1	860 6	1 006 3	588 5	119 4	16 0	--	--	--	--	1 8	3 209 6
Exotic hardwoods group	--	4 6	2 3	--	--	--	--	--	--	--	--	--	6 9
Nonstocked	155 6	--	--	--	--	--	--	--	--	--	--	--	156 1
All forest type groups	155 6	1 571 9	3 214 1	6 208 2	5 604 0	1 985 3	357 4	118 7	54 2	10 5	19 9	1 8	19 311 9

All table cells without observations in the inventory sample are indicated by -- Table value of 0 0 indicates the acres round to less than 0 1 thousand acres Columns and rows may not add to their totals due to rounding

Table 7.—Area of forest land, in thousand acres, by forest-type group and stand origin, Michigan, 2004

Forest type group	Stand origin		All forest land
	Natural stands	Artificial regeneration	
White / red / jack pine group	1 211 0	844 8	2 055 8
Spruce / fir group	2 530 4	50 2	2 580 7
Pinyon / juniper group	3 3	- -	3 3
Douglas-fir group	- -	4 5	4 5
Fir / spruce / mountain hemlock grou	- -	13 6	13 6
Exotic softwoods group	36 8	122 1	158 9
Oak / pine group	456 4	83 4	539 9
Oak / hickory group	2 557 1	34 0	2 591 1
Oak / gum / cypress group	56 6	- -	56 6
Elm / ash / cottonwood group	1 468 0	4 6	1 472 5
Maple / beech / birch group	6 423 6	38 8	6 462 5
Aspen / birch group	3 178 6	31 0	3 209 6
Exotic hardwoods group	6 9	- -	6 9
Nonstocked	150 6	5 5	156 1
All forest type groups	18 079 3	1 232 7	19 311 9

All table cells without observations in the inventory sample are indicated by -- Table value of 0 0 indicates the acres round to less than 0 1 thousand acres Columns and rows may not add to their totals due to rounding

Table 8.—Area of forest land, in thousand acres, by forest-type group and disturbance class, Michigan, 2004

Forest type group	Disturbance class									All forest land
	None	Insects	Disease	Weather	Fire	Domestic animals	Wild animals	Human	Other	
White / red / jack pine group	2 034 7	1 9	4 1	5 3	7 3	--	--	0 6	1 8	2 055 8
Spruce / fir group	2 552 4	--	--	8 4	--	--	10 8	7 1	1 9	2 580 7
Pinyon / juniper group	3 3	--	--	--	--	--	--	--	--	3 3
Douglas-fir group	4 5	--	--	--	--	--	--	--	--	4 5
Fir / spruce / mountain hemlock group	13 6	--	--	--	--	--	--	--	--	13 6
Exotic softwoods group	154 9	--	2 0	2 1	1 8	--	--	1 8	--	158 9
Oak / pine group	519 5	--	2 0	4 0	1 8	--	--	10 3	2 2	539 9
Oak / hickory group	2 540 9	0 5	3 4	11 0	4 9	1 7	4 7	22 1	1 9	2 591 1
Oak / gum / cypress group	53 0	--	--	1 8	--	--	--	1 8	--	56 6
Elm / ash / cottonwood group	1 428 2	0 5	--	21 6	--	--	10 3	4 0	7 9	1 472 5
Maple / beech / birch group	6 353 3	22 8	3 0	8 3	3 9	6 7	11 4	51 7	1 3	6 462 5
Aspen / birch group	3 142 4	8 6	--	15 2	4 1	2 6	15 0	21 8	--	3 209 6
Exotic hardwoods group	6 9	--	--	--	--	--	--	--	--	6 9
Nonstocked	148 7	--	--	--	--	--	1 1	6 3	--	156 1
All forest type groups	18 956 4	34 3	12 6	77 8	22 0	11 0	53 2	127 5	17 1	19 311 9

All table cells without observations in the inventory sample are indicated by -- Table value of 0 0 indicates the acres round to less than 0 1 thousand acres Columns and rows may not add to their totals due to rounding

54

Table 9.—Area of timberland, in thousand acres, by forest-type group and stand-size class, Michigan, 2004

Forest type group	Stand-size class					All size classes
	Large diameter	Medium diameter	Small diameter	Chaparral	Nonstocked	
White / red / jack pine group	989 6	685 9	271 1	--	--	1 946 6
Spruce / fir group	619 5	1 190 3	661 5	--	--	2 471 4
Pinyon / juniper group	--	1 1	2 1	--	--	3 3
Douglas-fir group	2 1	2 5	--	--	--	4 5
Fir / spruce / mountain hemlock grou	1 1	2 5	10 0	--	--	13 6
Exotic softwoods group	52 3	65 6	39 0	--	--	156 8
Oak / pine group	190 3	189 6	136 7	--	--	516 6
Oak / hickory group	1 488 2	713 8	368 5	--	--	2 570 5
Oak / gum / cypress group	25 3	23 9	7 4	--	--	56 6
Elm / ash / cottonwood group	541 6	573 5	331 5	--	--	1 446 6
Maple / beech / birch group	3 009 1	2 654 4	640 0	--	--	6 303 5
Aspen / birch group	583 0	1 380 1	1 134 7	--	--	3 097 8
Exotic hardwoods group	2 1	2 4	2 4	--	--	6 9
Nonstocked	--	--	0 5	--	150 3	150 9
All forest type groups	7 504 1	7 485 6	3 605 7	--	150 3	18 745 7

All table cells without observations in the inventory sample are indicated by -- Table value of 0 0 indicates the acres round to less than 0 1 thousand acres Columns and rows may not add to their totals due to rounding

55

Table 10.—Number of live trees (at least 1 inch d.b.h./d.r.c.), in thousand trees, on forest land by species group and diameter class, Michigan, 2004

Species group	1.0-2.9	3.0-4.9	5.0-6.9	7.0-8.9	9.0-10.9	11.0-12.9	13.0-14.9	15.0-16.9	17.0-18.9	19.0-20.9	21.0-24.9	25.0-28.9	29.0-32.9	33.0-36.9	37.0+	All classes
Softwood species groups																
Eastern softwood species groups																
Other yellow pines	14,016	15,747	11,508	7,441	4,501	1,749	424	237	70	--	--	--	--	--	--	55,693
Eastern white and red pines	182,372	103,946	99,396	84,887	54,036	29,461	15,784	8,800	4,759	3,047	2,561	962	285	59	24	590,380
Jack pine	121,488	70,345	46,695	30,907	14,532	5,339	1,523	427	135	24	--	--	--	--	--	291,416
Spruce and balsam fir	1,741,109	485,151	191,800	83,012	28,892	10,765	4,295	1,700	528	425	137	--	--	--	--	2,547,814
Eastern hemlock	49,792	28,907	15,613	13,368	10,616	8,416	6,625	4,754	3,495	2,077	1,817	527	136	23	23	146,190
Other eastern softwoods	464,898	324,134	224,099	136,372	70,624	32,250	14,813	6,790	2,562	1,124	662	203	74	12	23	1,278,615
All softwoods	2,573,676	1,028,230	589,112	355,987	183,201	87,980	43,464	22,707	11,549	6,697	5,177	1,692	495	94	47	4,910,109
Hardwood species groups																
Eastern hardwood species groups																
Select white oaks	58,550	27,103	17,775	13,082	9,687	7,204	4,446	2,714	2,095	1,293	1,040	428	133	106	80	145,735
Select red oaks	112,254	42,998	21,802	17,041	16,914	14,053	9,368	7,593	4,012	2,121	1,867	539	175	53	12	250,803
Other white oaks	--	--	--	12	--	--	28	--	--	--	--	--	--	--	--	40
Other red oaks	67,315	25,395	13,686	11,817	9,785	6,890	5,812	3,597	2,298	1,562	1,179	431	69	55	41	149,933
Hickory	27,073	9,477	5,205	3,574	2,105	1,839	1,089	706	299	260	148	13	--	27	--	51,816
Yellow birch	78,333	33,414	19,351	14,662	9,773	6,098	3,880	2,534	1,659	832	780	270	123	12	24	171,744
Hard maple	785,674	283,122	156,921	116,210	77,104	45,972	25,020	12,426	6,599	2,915	2,709	566	127	86	--	1,515,450
Soft maple	953,959	304,556	172,960	113,873	71,068	39,834	20,350	10,957	5,688	3,048	2,680	672	252	106	79	1,700,082
Beech	146,996	32,829	13,272	8,178	6,151	4,552	2,960	2,300	1,403	762	758	181	13	13	--	220,377
Tupelo and blackgum	4,416	838	716	523	265	96	55	26	28	--	--	--	--	--	--	6,963
Ash	550,352	176,174	78,923	39,898	22,153	12,337	7,374	3,596	1,732	781	606	190	53	13	--	894,181
Cottonwood and aspen	1,118,799	352,924	143,794	78,449	50,405	32,829	19,678	10,211	4,490	2,142	1,042	272	52	63	27	1,815,178
Basswood	50,333	19,679	14,363	14,964	13,090	10,274	5,973	2,924	1,267	664	421	88	62	--	13	134,115
Yellow-poplar	1,162	667	281	253	179	223	302	208	146	121	124	25	13	--	--	3,706
Black walnut	1,895	2,586	976	810	520	506	269	110	140	114	70	15	--	29	--	8,041
Other eastern soft hardwoods	583,545	192,421	98,763	59,996	34,356	19,886	8,848	4,200	2,095	1,066	566	167	56	26	27	1,006,017
Other eastern hard hardwoods	27,832	3,821	2,193	1,517	629	215	206	136	114	27	12	12	--	--	--	36,713
Eastern noncommercial hardwoods	673,288	90,345	19,997	5,964	1,525	586	147	62	15	--	12	--	--	--	--	791,940
All hardwoods	5,241,776	1,598,348	780,980	500,825	325,711	203,394	115,778	64,327	34,079	17,728	14,016	3,871	1,114	588	301	8,902,836
All species groups	7,815,452	2,626,578	1,370,092	856,812	508,912	291,374	159,241	87,034	45,627	24,425	19,194	5,563	1,609	682	349	13,812,944

All table cells without observations in the inventory sample are indicated by -- Table value of 0 indicates the number of trees rounds to less than 1 thousand trees Columns and rows may not add to their totals due to rounding

Table 11.—Number of growing-stock trees (at least 5 inches d.b.h.), in thousand trees, on timberland by species group and diameter class, Michigan, 2004

Species group	Diameter class (inches)													All classes
	5.0-6.9	7.0-8.9	9.0-10.9	11.0-12.9	13.0-14.9	15.0-16.9	17.0-18.9	19.0-20.9	21.0-24.9	25.0-28.9	29.0-32.9	33.0-36.9	37.0+	
Softwood species groups														
Eastern softwood species groups														
Other yellow pines	9 120	6 369	3 925	1 608	356	201	44	--	--	--	--	--	--	21 624
Eastern white and red pines	93 913	82 084	52 263	28 530	15 117	8 527	4 511	2 846	2 460	873	248	47	12	291 429
Jack pine	39 611	28 827	13 372	4 965	1 372	401	85	12	--	--	--	--	--	88 646
Spruce and balsam fir	183 253	78 893	27 204	9 990	3 826	1 480	493	388	125	--	--	--	--	305 654
Eastern hemlock	12 807	11 463	9 109	7 401	5 690	4 258	2 888	1 748	1 431	332	62	12	--	57 201
Other eastern softwoods	198 509	121 599	61 243	27 877	12 621	5 550	2 165	964	492	179	74	12	--	431 284
All softwoods	537 213	329 236	167 115	80 371	38 983	20 417	10 185	5 958	4 508	1 384	384	71	12	1 195 838
Hardwood species groups														
Eastern hardwood species groups														
Select white oaks	16 064	12 159	9 137	6 582	4 082	2 550	1 920	1 163	895	325	78	39	41	55 033
Select red oaks	19 660	15 884	16 180	13 312	8 508	7 072	3 797	1 938	1 550	449	122	53	--	88 524
Other white oaks	--	12	--	--	--	28	--	--	--	--	--	--	--	40
Other red oaks	11 096	10 204	8 741	5 971	5 075	3 160	2 143	1 431	1 040	379	42	26	28	49 337
Hickory	4 977	3 346	2 090	1 784	991	652	287	248	135	13	--	--	--	14 524
Yellow birch	15 659	12 530	8 039	4 871	2 951	2 003	1 115	615	479	146	62	12	12	48 496
Hard maple	145 222	108 961	72 382	42 370	22 973	11 162	5 698	2 362	2 014	355	37	62	--	413 598
Soft maple	157 358	104 594	65 288	34 849	17 902	9 636	4 909	2 648	1 975	455	187	53	39	399 892
Beech	11 612	7 110	5 301	3 712	2 207	1 715	1 088	522	525	26	--	--	--	33 818
Tupelo and blackgum	621	469	250	55	55	26	28	--	--	--	--	--	--	1 503
Ash	71 275	36 544	20 720	11 157	6 823	3 368	1 517	730	563	163	53	--	--	152 913
Cottonwood and aspen	137 031	74 122	47 413	29 373	17 731	8 713	3 853	1 830	868	245	39	49	13	321 282
Basswood	12 929	14 022	12 346	9 757	5 603	2 736	1 130	598	321	64	25	--	13	59 545
Yellow-poplar	256	253	166	210	302	195	146	108	124	25	13	--	--	1 799
Black walnut	843	727	478	407	230	81	140	85	41	15	--	29	--	3 076
Other eastern soft hardwoods	78 503	49 179	28 328	15 626	7 094	3 265	1 589	775	447	90	41	26	13	184 976
Other eastern hard hardwoods	1 513	1 086	411	123	93	121	71	27	12	12	--	--	--	3 471
All hardwoods	664 620	451 202	297 271	180 159	102 620	56 483	29 432	15 080	10 991	2 760	699	349	159	1 831 826
All species groups	1 221 833	780 438	464 387	260 531	141 603	76 900	39 617	21 038	15 499	4 144	1 083	420	171	3 027 663

All table cells without observations in the inventory sample are indicated by — Table value of 0 indicates the number of trees rounds to less than 1 thousand trees Columns and rows may not add to their totals due to rounding

Table 12.—Net volume of live trees (at least 5 inches d.b.h./d.r.c.), in million cubic feet, by owner class and forest-land status, Michigan, 2004

Owner class	Unreserved forests			Reserved forests			All forest land
	Timberland	Unproductive	Total	Productive	Unproductive	Total	
Forest Service							
National forest	4 598 1	34 5	4 632 6	207 1	0 2	207 3	4 839 9
Other national forest	17 9	--	17 9	--	--	--	17 9
Other Federal							
National Park Service	118 2	10 5	128 7	288 8	3 3	292 1	420 9
Fish and Wildlife Service	19 5	--	19 5	1 9	--	1 9	21 4
Department of Defense or Energy	17 4	--	17 4	--	--	--	17 4
Other Federal	33 7	--	33 7	--	--	--	33 7
State and local government							
State	5 477 5	21 4	5 498 8	250 4	--	250 4	5 749 3
Local (county municipal etc)	507 2	--	507 2	9 4	--	9 4	516 5
Other non-Federal lands	16 1	--	16 1	--	--	--	16 1
Private							
Undifferentiated private	18 477 9	100 9	18 578 8	29 7	3 1	32 8	18 611 6
All owners	29 283 5	167 2	29 450 7	787 3	6 6	793 9	30 244 6

All table cells without observations in the inventory sample are indicated by -- Table value of 0 0 indicates the volume rounds to less than 0 1 million cubic feet Columns and rows may not add to their totals due to rounding

Table 13.—Net volume of live trees (at least 5 inches d.b.h./d.r.c.), in million cubic feet, on forest land by forest-type group and stand-size class, Michigan, 2004

Forest type group	Stand-size class					All size classes
	Large diameter	Medium diameter	Small diameter	Chaparral	Nonstocked	
White / red / jack pine group	2 569 8	1 038 8	48 4	--	--	3 657 0
Spruce / fir group	1 485 1	2 000 1	243 9	--	--	3 729 1
Pinyon / juniper group	--	0 4	0 2	--	--	0 6
Douglas-fir group	1 6	4 0	--	--	--	5 6
Fir / spruce / mountain hemlock grou	1 8	3 6	0 5	--	--	5 9
Exotic softwoods group	117 0	83 1	5 5	--	--	205 5
Oak / pine group	366 1	265 7	33 9	--	--	665 7
Oak / hickory group	3 204 7	914 8	85 2	--	--	4 204 7
Oak / gum / cypress group	68 2	36 3	4 0	--	--	108 4
Elm / ash / cottonwood group	1 257 5	737 8	98 6	--	--	2 093 9
Maple / beech / birch group	7 430 8	4 325 0	177 1	--	--	11 932 9
Aspen / birch group	1 408 6	1 926 6	287 5	--	--	3 622 6
Exotic hardwoods group	0 8	1 7	--	--	--	2 5
Nonstocked	--	--	--	--	10 1	10 1
All forest type groups	17 912 0	11 337 8	984 7	--	10 1	30 244 6

All table cells without observations in the inventory sample are indicated by -- Table value of 0 0 indicates the volume rounds to less than 0 1 million cubic feet Columns and rows may not add to their totals due to rounding

59

Table 14.—Net volume of live trees (at least 5 inches d.b.h./d.r.c.), in million cubic feet, on forest land by species group and ownership group, Michigan, 2004

Species group	Ownership group				
	Forest Service	Other Federal	State and local government	Undifferentiated private	All owners
Softwood species groups					
Eastern softwood species groups					
Other yellow pines	1 2	0 2	4 5	150 0	155 9
Eastern white and red pines	969 6	27 3	913 9	1 365 7	3 276 5
Jack pine	160 8	9 9	205 3	151 7	527 7
Spruce and balsam fir	340 7	50 1	383 6	926 5	1 700 9
Eastern hemlock	192 1	12 9	169 7	530 5	905 1
Other eastern softwoods	423 4	75 4	800 3	1 616 4	2 915 4
All softwoods	2 087 8	175 8	2 477 3	4 740 8	9 481 6
Hardwood species groups					
Eastern hardwood species groups					
Select white oaks	100 0	3 9	151 4	542 7	798 1
Select red oaks	170 6	22 0	343 8	968 4	1 504 7
Other white oaks	--	--	--	0 8	0 8
Other red oaks	123 3	5 9	159 0	518 1	806 4
Hickory	--	0 8	22 0	167 2	190 0
Yellow birch	144 2	30 7	102 2	387 0	664 1
Hard maple	731 2	70 7	731 9	3 008 0	4 541 7
Soft maple	562 6	24 8	723 5	2 819 1	4 130 0
Beech	74 4	31 4	92 9	325 8	524 5
Tupelo and blackgum	--	--	1 5	10 2	11 7
Ash	93 4	7 6	218 3	1 047 5	1 366 8
Cottonwood and aspen	464 0	52 2	716 3	2 009 1	3 241 6
Basswood	110 4	5 9	183 3	541 2	840 8
Yellow-poplar	--	--	5 8	50 8	56 6
Black walnut	--	--	5 9	53 7	59 5
Other eastern soft hardwoods	189 9	60 2	332 8	1 319 3	1 902 1
Other eastern hard hardwoods	--	--	1 7	32 6	34 2
Eastern noncommercial hardwoods	5 9	1 5	12 4	69 3	89 2
All hardwoods	2 769 9	317 6	3 804 6	13 870 9	20 763 0
All species groups	4 857 7	493 4	6 281 9	18 611 6	30 244 6

All table cells without observations in the inventory sample are indicated by -- Table value of 0 0 indicates the volume rounds to less than 0 1 million cubic feet Columns and rows may not add to their totals due to rounding

Table 15.—Net volume of live trees (at least 5 inches d.b.h./d.r.c.), in million cubic feet, on forest land by species group and diameter class, Michigan, 2004

						Diameter class (inches)							
Species group	5.0-6.9	7.0-8.9	9.0-10.9	11.0-12.9	13.0-14.9	15.0-16.9	17.0-18.9	19.0-20.9	21.0-24.9	25.0-28.9	29.0-32.9	33.0-36.9	37.0+	All classes
Softwood species groups														
Eastern softwood species groups														
Other yellow pines	26	39	43	28	10	8	3	--	--	--	--	--	--	156
Eastern white and red pines	252	482	547	480	379	300	221	187	220	130	53	16	10	3 276
Jack pine	104	157	133	79	34	14	6	1	--	--	--	--	--	528
Spruce and balsam fir	496	483	304	184	111	60	25	26	11	--	--	--	--	1 701
Eastern hemlock	24	51	78	102	122	125	125	94	111	45	18	4	5	905
Other eastern softwoods	514	676	615	436	290	180	89	50	39	16	8	2	--	2 915
All softwoods	1 416	1 888	1 720	1 310	947	686	469	359	380	191	79	22	15	9 482
Hardwood species groups														
Eastern hardwood species groups														
Select white oaks	41	66	88	104	94	79	82	67	71	45	17	18	25	798
Select red oaks	50	91	164	216	210	241	176	118	143	59	26	10	3	1 505
Other white oaks	--	0	--	--	--	1	--	--	--	--	--	--	--	1
Other red oaks	30	60	87	99	119	102	87	76	77	42	10	8	12	806
Hickory	11	19	22	32	28	25	15	17	12	2	--	7	--	190
Yellow birch	48	81	96	92	82	73	60	38	49	23	14	2	6	664
Hard maple	432	714	843	784	618	417	287	163	192	57	17	18	--	4 542
Soft maple	456	676	749	653	484	355	246	168	196	67	35	20	23	4 130
Beech	36	49	65	74	67	70	57	40	50	15	--	2	--	524
Tupelo and blackgum	2	3	3	1	1	1	1	--	--	--	--	--	--	12
Ash	196	227	231	205	180	122	77	46	49	22	9	1	--	1 367
Cottonwood and aspen	384	474	547	558	490	343	193	120	77	29	7	12	7	3 242
Basswood	39	92	143	175	149	98	56	37	30	9	8	--	5	841
Yellow-poplar	1	2	2	4	9	8	7	8	11	3	2	--	--	57
Black walnut	3	6	6	9	7	4	6	6	5	2	--	5	--	60
Other eastern soft hardwoods	261	358	367	334	214	139	91	59	41	16	7	5	10	1 902
Other eastern hard hardwoods	5	7	5	3	4	4	4	1	1	1	--	--	--	34
Eastern noncommercial hardwoods	39	26	12	7	2	2	1	--	--	--	--	--	--	89
All hardwoods	2 034	2 951	3 430	3 350	2 757	2 084	1 446	964	1 004	393	152	106	90	20 763
All species groups	3 450	4 840	5 150	4 660	3 705	2 771	1 915	1 323	1 384	584	231	128	105	30 245

All table cells without observations in the inventory sample are indicated by — Table value of 0 indicates the volume rounds to less than 1 million cubic feet. Columns and rows may not add to their totals due to rounding

61

Table 16.—Net volume of live trees (at least 5 inches d.b.h./d.r.c.), in million cubic feet, on forest land by forest-type group and stand origin, Michigan, 2004

Forest type group	Stand origin		All forest land
	Natural stands	Artificial regeneration	
White / red / jack pine group	2 013 6	1 643 4	3 657 0
Spruce / fir group	3 669 0	60 1	3 729 1
Pinyon / juniper group	0 6	- -	0 6
Douglas-fir group	- -	5 6	5 6
Fir / spruce / mountain hemlock grou	- -	5 9	5 9
Exotic softwoods group	41 1	164 4	205 5
Oak / pine group	580 8	84 9	665 7
Oak / hickory group	4 170 7	33 9	4 204 7
Oak / gum / cypress group	108 4	- -	108 4
Elm / ash / cottonwood group	2 090 8	3 2	2 093 9
Maple / beech / birch group	11 901 3	31 6	11 932 9
Aspen / birch group	3 591 1	31 6	3 622 6
Exotic hardwoods group	2 5	- -	2 5
Nonstocked	10 1	- -	10 1
All forest type groups	28 180 0	2 064 7	30 244 6

All table cells without observations in the inventory sample are indicated by — Table value of 0 0 indicates the volume rounds to less than 0 1 million cubic feet Columns and rows may not add to their totals due to rounding

Table 17.—Net volume of growing-stock trees (at least 5 inches d.b.h.), in million cubic feet, on timberland by species group and diameter class, Michigan, 2004

| Species group | \multicolumn{14}{c}{Diameter class (inches)} | | | | | | | | | | | | | |
	5.0-6.9	7.0-8.9	9.0-10.9	11.0-12.9	13.0-14.9	15.0-16.9	17.0-18.9	19.0-20.9	21.0-24.9	25.0-28.9	29.0-32.9	33.0-36.9	37.0+	All classes
Softwood species groups														
Eastern softwood species groups														
Other yellow pines	22	35	38	26	9	7	2	--	--	--	--	--	--	138
Eastern white and red pines	241	469	531	467	364	291	211	176	212	118	45	13	5	3 142
Jack pine	91	149	124	74	31	13	4	1	--	--	--	--	--	487
Spruce and balsam fir	475	460	287	171	99	52	24	24	10	--	--	--	--	1 602
Eastern hemlock	20	45	68	91	107	113	104	80	88	29	8	2	--	757
Other eastern softwoods	466	616	548	389	255	153	78	45	30	15	8	2	--	2 604
All softwoods	1 315	1 772	1 597	1 218	866	629	423	325	341	161	61	17	5	8 729
Hardwood species groups														
Eastern hardwood species groups														
Select white oaks	37	62	84	97	87	75	76	60	63	36	10	8	15	711
Select red oaks	46	86	158	205	193	227	168	109	121	50	19	10	--	1 391
Other white oaks	--	0	--	--	--	1	--	--	--	--	--	--	--	1
Other red oaks	25	53	79	87	105	92	82	70	69	37	6	5	9	717
Hickory	11	18	22	31	26	23	14	16	11	2	--	--	--	175
Yellow birch	40	71	80	76	65	60	42	30	31	13	8	2	3	520
Hard maple	404	675	797	730	573	380	252	135	148	38	6	13	3	4 150
Soft maple	422	630	698	585	435	320	218	149	151	49	28	12	15	3 710
Beech	32	44	57	62	53	55	47	29	39	3	--	--	--	422
Tupelo and blackgum	1	3	3	1	1	1	1	--	--	--	--	--	--	11
Ash	181	212	219	189	169	116	69	44	47	19	9	--	--	1 273
Cottonwood and aspen	370	454	522	514	455	307	175	107	68	27	6	10	4	3 020
Basswood	36	87	136	168	140	93	50	34	23	7	4	--	5	783
Yellow-poplar	1	2	2	4	9	7	7	7	11	3	2	--	--	55
Black walnut	3	5	6	8	6	3	6	5	3	2	--	5	--	52
Other eastern soft hardwoods	212	300	309	271	177	113	73	45	35	10	6	5	2	1 558
Other eastern hard hardwoods	4	6	4	2	2	3	3	1	1	1	--	--	--	26
All hardwoods	1 824	2 706	3 175	3 029	2 495	1 878	1 284	841	820	298	104	69	52	18 574
All species groups	3 139	4 478	4 772	4 248	3 361	2 507	1 707	1 166	1 161	459	165	86	56	27 303

All table cells without observations in the inventory sample are indicated by -- Table value of 0 indicates the volume rounds to less than 1 million cubic feet Columns and rows may not add to their totals due to rounding

Table 18.—Net volume of growing-stock trees (at least 5 inches d.b.h.), in million cubic feet, on timberland by species group and ownership group, Michigan, 2004

Species group	Ownership group				All owners
	Forest Service	Other Federal	State and local government	Undifferentiated private	
Softwood species groups					
Eastern softwood species groups					
Other yellow pines	0 3	--	4 3	133 3	137 9
Eastern white and red pines	928 8	9 7	886 6	1 317 3	3 142 4
Jack pine	151 5	7 3	188 0	139 9	486 8
Spruce and balsam fir	316 7	7 5	372 3	905 3	1 601 8
Eastern hemlock	163 5	6 2	91 3	495 7	756 7
Other eastern softwoods	373 0	14 1	738 8	1 477 8	2 603 7
All softwoods	1 933 9	44 7	2 281 4	4 469 3	8 729 3
Hardwood species groups					
Eastern hardwood species groups					
Select white oaks	92 2	3 0	127 7	488 4	711 2
Select red oaks	154 5	12 7	308 4	915 1	1 390 6
Other white oaks	--	--	--	0 8	0 8
Other red oaks	108 7	3 9	142 4	462 2	717 2
Hickory	--	0 8	20 1	153 8	174 8
Yellow birch	108 0	7 4	69 8	335 0	520 3
Hard maple	651 6	38 6	630 5	2 829 0	4 149 6
Soft maple	499 6	19 5	643 4	2 547 3	3 709 8
Beech	59 4	19 1	77 8	265 5	421 8
Tupelo and blackgum	--	--	1 5	9 3	10 7
Ash	85 5	1 5	199 6	986 7	1 273 2
Cottonwood and aspen	426 8	12 6	669 6	1 911 1	3 020 1
Basswood	108 0	1 8	161 7	511 6	783 2
Yellow-poplar	--	--	5 8	49 3	55 1
Black walnut	--	--	5 7	45 8	51 6
Other eastern soft hardwoods	161 9	9 4	272 9	1 114 3	1 558 3
Other eastern hard hardwoods	--	--	1 2	24 4	25 6
All hardwoods	2 456 1	130 2	3 338 0	12 649 6	18 573 8
All species groups	4 390 0	174 9	5 619 4	17 118 9	27 303 2

All table cells without observations in the inventory sample are indicated by — Table value of 0 0 indicates the volume rounds to less than 0 1 million cubic feet Columns and rows may not add to their totals due to rounding

Table 19.—Net volume of sawtimber trees, in million board feet (International ¼-inch rule), on timberland by species group and diameter class, Michigan, 2004

Species group	Diameter class (inches)											All classes
	9.0-10.9	11.0-12.9	13.0-14.9	15.0-16.9	17.0-18.9	19.0-20.9	21.0-24.9	25.0-28.9	29.0-32.9	33.0-36.9	37.0+	
Softwood species groups												
Eastern softwood species groups												
Other yellow pines	181	126	46	37	11	--	--	--	--	--	--	400
Eastern white and red pines	2 619	2 348	1 878	1 540	1 142	973	1 202	688	265	80	29	12 762
Jack pine	593	365	161	70	21	4	--	--	--	--	--	1 214
Spruce and balsam fir	1 430	884	530	289	135	137	60	--	--	--	--	3 465
Eastern hemlock	330	442	536	587	558	441	502	168	49	12	--	3 625
Other eastern softwoods	2 737	1 970	1 327	819	428	250	175	86	49	12	--	7 852
All softwoods	7 889	6 134	4 478	3 340	2 294	1 805	1 938	942	363	104	29	29 317
Hardwood species groups												
Eastern hardwood species groups												
Select white oaks	--	395	379	343	356	291	312	184	54	43	82	2 439
Select red oaks	--	833	840	1 034	790	528	603	258	100	54	--	5 040
Other white oaks	--	--	--	3	--	--	--	--	--	--	--	3
Other red oaks	--	358	463	421	389	340	348	194	29	26	49	2 617
Hickory	--	113	104	102	64	77	54	10	--	--	--	524
Yellow birch	--	330	303	292	213	154	162	72	46	12	15	1 599
Hard maple	--	3 021	2 562	1 775	1 216	665	747	196	30	72	--	10 286
Soft maple	--	2 383	1 916	1 476	1 038	725	756	252	151	64	83	8 843
Beech	--	275	249	274	237	153	206	18	--	--	--	1 412
Tupelo and blackgum	--	3	6	4	6	--	--	--	--	--	--	18
Ash	--	784	749	535	331	212	235	100	49	--	--	2 996
Cottonwood and aspen	--	2 181	2 062	1 451	845	528	344	140	33	52	21	7 656
Basswood	--	707	634	437	244	169	116	37	19	--	26	2 389
Yellow-poplar	--	17	39	35	36	35	59	19	9	--	--	248
Black walnut	--	32	29	15	31	26	16	9	--	25	--	184
Other eastern soft hardwoods	--	1 101	777	519	346	218	172	54	34	25	13	3 261
Other eastern hard hardwoods	--	7	9	16	12	6	4	5	--	--	--	59
All hardwoods	--	12 542	11 121	8 731	6 152	4 126	4 135	1 549	555	373	289	49 574
All species groups	7 889	18 675	15 600	12 072	8 446	5 931	6 073	2 492	918	477	318	78 891

All table cells without observations in the inventory sample are indicated by -- Table value of 0 indicates the volume rounds to less than 1 million board feet Columns and rows may not add to their totals due to rounding

Table 19a.—Net volume of sawtimber trees, in million board feet (Doyle rule), on timberland by species group and diameter class, Michigan, 2004

Species group	Diameter class (inches)											All classes
	9.0-10.9	11.0-12.9	13.0-14.9	15.0-16.9	17.0-18.9	19.0-20.9	21.0-24.9	25.0-28.9	29.0-32.9	33.0-36.9	37.0+	
Softwood species groups												
Eastern softwood species groups												
Other yellow pines	62	60	28	25	8	--	--	--	--	--	--	184
Eastern white and red pines	905	1 122	1 125	1 064	878	834	1 070	660	293	88	33	8 071
Jack pine	205	175	96	48	16	3	--	--	--	--	--	544
Spruce and balsam fir	494	422	318	200	104	117	53	--	--	--	--	1 708
Eastern hemlock	114	211	321	405	429	378	445	161	54	14	--	2 532
Other eastern softwoods	946	942	795	566	329	214	156	82	54	14	--	4 097
All softwoods	2 726	2 932	2 683	2 307	1 763	1 547	1 724	903	401	116	33	17 135
Hardwood species groups												
Eastern hardwood species groups												
Select white oaks	--	165	194	202	234	209	251	170	61	49	93	1 627
Select red oaks	--	347	430	608	519	379	484	231	114	61	--	3 173
Other white oaks	--	--	--	2	--	--	--	--	--	--	--	2
Other red oaks	--	149	237	248	255	244	280	176	33	30	56	1 707
Hickory	--	47	53	60	42	55	43	10	--	--	--	309
Yellow birch	--	138	155	172	140	111	130	65	53	14	17	992
Hard maple	--	1 260	1 311	1 044	799	478	598	179	34	82	--	5 786
Soft maple	--	994	980	868	682	520	608	225	172	72	94	5 215
Beech	--	115	128	161	156	110	166	16	--	--	--	851
Tupelo and blackgum	--	1	3	2	4	--	--	--	--	--	--	10
Ash	--	327	384	315	218	152	190	92	56	--	--	1 733
Cottonwood and aspen	--	910	1 055	854	555	379	276	127	37	59	24	4 275
Basswood	--	295	325	257	160	121	93	33	22	--	29	1 335
Yellow-poplar	--	7	20	21	23	25	47	16	10	--	--	170
Black walnut	--	13	15	9	20	19	13	9	--	29	--	126
Other eastern soft hardwoods	--	459	398	305	227	157	138	49	39	29	15	1 816
Other eastern hard hardwoods	--	3	4	9	8	4	3	5	--	--	--	37
All hardwoods	--	5 232	5 692	5 136	4 041	2 962	3 319	1 402	630	423	328	29 166
All species groups	2 726	8 164	8 375	7 443	5 805	4 510	5 043	2 305	1 031	539	360	46 301

All table cells without observations in the inventory sample are indicated by -- Table value of 0 indicates the volume rounds to less than 1 million board feet Columns and rows may not add to their totals due to rounding

66

Table 20.—Net volume of saw-log portion of sawtimber trees, in million cubic feet, on timberland by species group and ownership group, Michigan, 2004

Species group	Ownership group				
	Forest Service	Other Federal	State and local government	Undifferentiated private	All owners
Softwood species groups					
Eastern softwood species groups					
Other yellow pines	0 2	--	2 1	67 1	69 4
Eastern white and red pines	642 3	7 0	646 3	865 3	2 161 0
Jack pine	58 2	2 9	79 7	68 2	209 0
Spruce and balsam fir	132 0	3 9	127 5	327 2	590 6
Eastern hemlock	135 0	5 1	70 7	394 6	605 4
Other eastern softwoods	203 0	9 8	342 9	751 9	1 307 7
All softwoods	1 170 8	28 7	1 269 2	2 474 3	4 943 1
Hardwood species groups					
Eastern hardwood species groups					
Select white oaks	43 7	1 0	64 1	276 8	385 7
Select red oaks	90 1	7 5	173 7	531 9	803 1
Other white oaks	--	--	--	0 6	0 6
Other red oaks	55 8	1 9	83 1	274 3	415 2
Hickory	--	0 2	10 1	73 2	83 5
Yellow birch	63 9	4 9	31 4	150 8	251 1
Hard maple	268 8	17 9	247 7	1 090 6	1 625 0
Soft maple	172 5	7 1	229 5	980 6	1 389 7
Beech	30 8	11 5	41 3	136 8	220 4
Tupelo and blackgum	--	--	0 5	2 5	3 0
Ash	28 3	0 8	73 0	380 5	482 6
Cottonwood and aspen	183 2	6 6	235 5	803 6	1 228 9
Basswood	55 0	0 8	79 4	246 9	382 2
Yellow-poplar	--	--	4 3	34 6	38 9
Black walnut	--	--	2 0	26 8	28 8
Other eastern soft hardwoods	54 5	4 5	81 9	375 5	516 4
Other eastern hard hardwoods	--	--	--	9 6	9 6
All hardwoods	1 046 7	64 9	1 357 6	5 395 6	7 864 8
All species groups	2 217 4	93 6	2 626 9	7 869 9	12 807 8

All table cells without observations in the inventory sample are indicated by -- Table value of 0 0 indicates the volume rounds to less than 0 1 million cubic feet Columns and rows may not add to their totals due to rounding

Table 24.—Average annual net growth of growing-stock trees (at least 5 inches d.b.h.), in million cubic feet, on timberland by species group and ownership group, Michigan, 1993 to 2004

Species group	Ownership group				
	Forest Service	Other Federal	State and local government	Undifferentiated private	All owners
Softwood species groups					
Eastern softwood species groups					
Other yellow pines	—	—	0.1	9.2	9.3
Eastern white and red pines	25.7	0.3	27.7	66.5	120.1
Jack pine	3.7	0.9	4.7	2.7	12.0
Spruce and balsam fir	7.2	0.1	11.2	27.0	45.5
Eastern hemlock	1.9	—	3.7	8.3	13.9
Other eastern softwoods	7.2	—	15.6	37.6	60.4
All softwoods	45.6	1.3	62.9	151.3	261.1
Hardwood species groups					
Eastern hardwood species groups					
Select white oaks	1.5	—	1.8	12.7	15.9
Select red oaks	4.0	—	5.7	33.0	42.7
Other red oaks	1.1	—	2.4	16.9	20.4
Hickory	—	—	1.8	4.7	6.5
Yellow birch	1.2	0.0	0.2	2.5	3.9
Hard maple	13.6	0.1	18.4	64.8	96.9
Soft maple	12.7	0.2	19.3	89.3	121.6
Beech	2.8	1.1	3.7	6.4	14.0
Tupelo and blackgum	—	—	—	0.1	0.1
Ash	1.5	—	4.6	39.6	45.8
Cottonwood and aspen	9.1	0.1	30.5	62.8	102.5
Basswood	0.8	—	0.0	7.7	8.4
Yellow-poplar	—	—	1.8	1.9	3.7
Black walnut	—	—	0.3	3.3	3.6
Other eastern soft hardwoods	0.9	—	5.5	31.3	37.8
Other eastern hard hardwoods	—	—	0.0	2.0	2.0
All hardwoods	49.0	1.5	96.1	379.0	525.7
All species groups	94.7	2.8	159.0	530.3	786.8

A table cell without observations in the inventory sample are indicated by —. Table value of 0.0 indicates the volume rounds to less than 0.1 million cubic feet. Columns and rows may not add to the row totals due to rounding.

Table 28.—Average annual mortality of growing-stock trees (at least 5 inches d.b.h.), in million cubic feet, on timberland by species group and ownership group, Michigan, 1993 to 2004

Species group	Ownership group				All owners
	Forest Service	Other Federal	State and local government	Undifferentiated private	
Softwood species groups					
Eastern softwood species groups					
Other yellow pines	--	--	0.4	2.8	3.1
Eastern white and red pines	3.6	--	2.8	2.2	8.7
Jack pine	3.8	0.6	2.9	1.9	9.1
Spruce and balsam fir	6.5	--	10.3	17.7	34.5
Eastern hemlock	0.7	--	0.3	1.5	2.4
Other eastern softwoods	2.7	--	4.3	4.6	11.6
All softwoods	17.3	0.6	20.9	30.6	69.5
Hardwood species groups					
Eastern hardwood species groups					
Select white oaks	0.1	--	0.7	2.4	3.2
Select red oaks	--	--	3.1	5.9	9.0
Other red oaks	1.8	--	0.5	1.8	4.1
Hickory	--	--	--	0.4	0.4
Yellow birch	0.7	--	0.6	2.3	3.6
Hard maple	2.1	--	2.2	7.2	11.5
Soft maple	1.3	--	3.3	9.9	14.5
Beech	--	--	--	0.7	0.7
Ash	1.0	--	1.0	4.6	6.6
Cottonwood and aspen	7.8	--	16.4	39.2	63.4
Basswood	0.7	--	1.8	1.8	4.3
Black walnut	--	--	--	0.4	0.4
Other eastern soft hardwoods	2.3	--	5.9	25.3	33.6
Other eastern hard hardwoods	--	--	--	--	--
All hardwoods	17.8	--	35.5	101.8	155.1
All species groups	35.1	0.6	56.4	132.5	224.5

All table cells without observations in the inventory sample are indicated by -- Table value of 0 0 indicates the volume rounds to less than 0 1 million cubic feet Columns and rows may not add to their totals due to rounding

Table 30.—Average annual removals of growing-stock trees (at least 5 inches d.b.h.), in million cubic feet, on timberland by species group and ownership group, Michigan, 1993 to 2004

Species group	Ownership group				
	Forest Service	Other Federal	State and local government	Undifferentiated private	All owners
Softwood species groups					
Eastern softwood species groups					
Other yellow pines	- -	- -	1 4	6 8	8 2
Eastern white and red pines	9 5	- -	9 3	9 8	28 6
Jack pine	2 0	- -	10 5	1 9	14 4
Spruce and balsam fir	0 5	- -	6 0	16 1	22 6
Eastern hemlock	0 1	- -	0 7	2 4	3 3
Other eastern softwoods	1 0	- -	0 9	9 0	10 9
All softwoods	13 2	- -	28 8	46 0	88 0
Hardwood species groups					
Eastern hardwood species groups					
Select white oaks	0 1	- -	0 8	3 1	4 0
Select red oaks	0 9	- -	3 6	13 4	17 9
Other red oaks	0 4	- -	0 9	2 3	3 6
Hickory	- -	- -	- -	0 8	0 8
Yellow birch	0 7	- -	0 4	1 3	2 5
Hard maple	4 9	- -	3 5	27 6	36 0
Soft maple	3 4	- -	6 3	17 9	27 6
Beech	0 6	- -	0 3	6 3	7 2
Ash	0 5	- -	1 0	5 7	7 1
Cottonwood and aspen	3 5	- -	14 7	48 5	66 7
Basswood	1 2	- -	1 3	4 4	6 9
Yellow-poplar	- -	- -	- -	1 1	1 1
Black walnut	- -	- -	- -	0 3	0 3
Other eastern soft hardwoods	0 6	- -	3 6	16 7	20 9
Other eastern hard hardwoods	- -	- -	- -	0 7	0 7
All hardwoods	16 9	- -	36 4	150 0	203 3
All species groups	30 0	- -	65 1	196 1	291 2

All table cells without observations in the inventory sample are indicated by -- Table value of 0 0 indicates the volume rounds to less than 0 1 million cubic feet Columns and rows may not add to their totals due to rounding

70

Table 31.—Aboveground dry weight of live trees (at least 1 inch d.b.h./d.r.c.), in thousand dry short tons, by owner class and forest-land status, Michigan, 2004

Owner class	Unreserved forests			Reserved forests			All forest land
	Timberland	Unproductive	Total	Productive	Unproductive	Total	
Forest Service							
National forest	113 833	910	114 743	5 140	11	5 150	119 893
Other national forest	453	--	453	--	--	--	453
Other Federal							
National Park Service	3 192	224	3 416	6 802	80	6 881	10 297
Fish and Wildlife Service	403	5	408	39	--	39	446
Department of Defense or Energy	471	--	471	--	--	--	471
Other Federal	969	--	969	--	--	--	969
State and local government							
State	139 923	666	140 588	6 345	--	6 345	146 934
Local (county municipal etc)	13 901	0	13 901	237	--	237	14 138
Other non-Federal lands	431	--	431	--	--	--	431
Private							
Undifferentiated private	496 224	2 606	498 830	766	68	835	499 665
All owners	769 800	4 410	774 210	19 328	159	19 487	793 697

All table cells without observations in the inventory sample are indicated by -- Table value of 0 indicates the aboveground tree biomass rounds to less than 1 thousand dry tons Columns and rows may not add to their totals due to rounding

Table 32.—Aboveground dry weight of live trees (at least 1 inch d.b.h./d.r.c.), in thousand dry short tons, on forest land by species group and diameter class, Michigan, 2004

Species group	1.0-2.9	3.0-4.9	5.0-6.9	7.0-8.9	9.0-10.9	11.0-12.9	13.0-14.9	15.0-16.9	17.0-18.9	19.0-20.9	21.0-22.9	23.0-24.9	25.0-26.9	27.0-28.9	29.0+	All classes
Softwood species groups																
Eastern softwood species groups																
Other yellow pines	46	271	570	810	858	532	197	146	59	--	--	--	--	--	--	3,490
Eastern white and red pines	439	1,559	4,557	8,393	9,368	8,141	6,376	5,016	3,704	3,118	2,190	1,447	1,136	1,007	1,307	57,757
Jack pine	304	938	1,944	2,819	2,341	1,368	591	236	100	21	--	--	--	--	--	10,663
Spruce and balsam fir	4,545	7,850	9,665	8,913	5,408	3,173	1,868	986	408	416	136	39	--	--	--	43,405
Eastern hemlock	98	337	587	1,166	1,697	2,159	2,533	2,529	2,489	1,859	1,418	753	560	313	497	18,996
Other eastern softwoods	1,217	4,481	8,905	11,055	9,775	6,761	4,384	2,678	1,320	717	319	243	170	52	135	52,212
All softwoods	6,649	15,435	26,228	33,156	29,447	22,135	15,949	11,591	8,079	6,132	4,062	2,481	1,866	1,373	1,939	186,522
Hardwood species groups																
Eastern hardwood species groups																
Select white oaks	267	754	1,468	2,262	2,887	3,354	2,950	2,455	2,500	2,008	1,210	934	517	824	1,811	26,201
Select red oaks	455	1,090	1,684	2,901	5,034	6,470	6,200	6,984	5,009	3,334	2,339	1,655	1,153	501	1,098	45,908
Other white oaks	--	--	--	2	--	--	--	24	--	--	--	--	--	--	--	26
Other red oaks	266	577	1,032	1,960	2,753	3,040	3,599	3,042	2,526	2,185	1,316	906	692	499	861	25,252
Hickory	98	226	408	651	697	995	861	769	430	502	315	40	--	54	214	6,260
Yellow birch	371	928	1,603	2,555	2,916	2,765	2,430	2,138	1,751	1,109	783	598	421	233	623	21,225
Hard maple	3,680	8,220	13,933	21,893	25,032	22,755	17,606	11,748	8,005	4,500	3,370	1,930	861	698	964	145,195
Soft maple	3,599	7,463	13,103	18,443	19,803	16,985	12,313	8,930	6,126	4,108	2,869	1,975	1,184	469	1,960	119,332
Beech	564	908	1,159	1,509	1,934	2,174	1,979	2,028	1,626	1,163	770	668	234	296	64	17,077
Tupelo and blackgum	16	18	45	77	66	34	33	18	28	--	--	--	--	--	--	335
Ash	2,026	4,046	5,597	6,247	6,227	5,469	4,719	3,160	2,029	1,172	654	592	265	292	282	42,778
Cottonwood and aspen	3,527	6,766	8,569	10,123	11,346	11,451	9,903	6,980	3,915	2,378	998	545	355	205	499	77,559
Basswood	149	347	787	1,749	2,626	3,135	2,608	1,702	968	632	297	212	90	71	207	15,569
Yellow-poplar	6	15	16	40	44	92	177	161	148	151	139	84	68	--	33	1,174
Black walnut	9	67	89	152	168	239	186	101	155	166	98	23	--	40	107	1,602
Other eastern soft hardwoods	2,115	4,510	7,173	9,361	9,298	8,268	5,181	3,310	2,134	1,333	620	302	217	155	464	54,442
Other eastern hard hardwoods	75	67	128	189	130	69	92	86	88	26	18	--	--	--	--	990
Eastern noncommercial hardwoods	1,914	1,728	1,190	754	332	195	65	39	14	--	--	18	--	--	--	6,249
All hardwoods	19,137	37,729	57,963	80,868	91,294	87,490	70,903	53,676	37,442	24,768	15,797	10,484	6,079	4,339	9,186	607,174
All species groups	25,787	53,165	84,211	114,024	120,741	109,625	86,851	65,267	45,521	30,900	19,859	12,965	7,945	5,712	11,125	793,697

All table cells without observations in the inventory sample are indicated by -- Table value of 0 indicates the aboveground tree biomass rounds to less than 1 thousand dry tons Columns and rows may not add to their totals due to rounding

Table 54.—Area of forest land, in thousand acres, by forest inventory unit, county, and forest-land status, Michigan, 2004

Forest Survey Unit and county	Unreserved forests			Reserved forests			All forest land
	Timberland	Unproductive	Total	Productive	Unproductive	Total	
Eastern Upper Peninsula							
Alger	523 7	6 5	530 2	6 5	- -	6 5	536 7
Chippewa	783 6	20 3	803 8	2 2	- -	2 2	806 0
Delta	591 6	6 5	598 1	- -	1 8	1 8	599 9
Luce	476 8	11 9	488 7	5 0	- -	5 0	493 6
Mackinac	560 2	13 6	573 8	8 7	0 7	9 4	583 3
Menominee	514 0	1 8	515 8	- -	- -	- -	515 8
Schoolcraft	558 8	11 5	570 3	6 2	- -	6 2	576 5
Total	4 008 6	72 2	4 080 8	28 6	2 6	31 1	4 111 9
Western Upper Peninsula							
Baraga	520 3	4 7	525 0	10 5	- -	10 5	535 5
Dickinson	407 3	- -	407 3	- -	- -	- -	407 3
Gogebic	616 3	5 7	621 9	33 8	- -	33 8	655 7
Houghton	515 9	- -	515 9	16 7	- -	16 7	532 6
ron	658 7	8 5	667 2	- -	- -	- -	667 2
Keweenaw	198 9	12 1	211 0	109 6	3 8	113 4	324 5
Marquette	993 0	19 5	1 012 5	14 7	- -	14 7	1 027 2
Ontonagon	670 1	15 8	685 9	55 0	- -	55 0	740 9
Total	4 580 5	66 1	4 646 6	240 2	3 8	244 1	4 890 7

(Table 54 continued on next page)

73

(Table 54 continued)

Forest Survey Unit and county	Unreserved forests			Reserved forests			All
	Timberland	Unproductive	Total	Productive	Unproductive	Total	forest land
Northern Lower Peninsula							
Alcona	317 3	3 1	320 4	--	--	--	320 4
Alpena	261 0	4 3	265 3	--	--	--	265 3
Antrim	183 1	--	183 1	--	--	--	183 1
Arenac	103 5	2 0	105 5	--	--	--	105 5
Bay	35 2	--	35 2	--	--	--	35 2
Benzie	132 8	--	132 8	5 8	--	5 8	138 7
Charlevoix	173 7	--	173 7	--	--	--	173 7
Cheboygan	362 7	5 8	368 6	--	--	--	368 6
Clare	190 9	0 1	190 9	--	--	--	190 9
Crawford	291 2	11 0	302 2	--	--	--	302 2
Emmet	215 7	--	215 7	2 0	--	2 0	217 8
Gladwin	192 4	--	192 4	2 0	--	2 0	194 4
Grand Traverse	167 1	6 1	173 3	1 3	--	1 3	174 6
osco	250 7	5 9	256 6	--	--	--	256 6
sabella	103 0	--	103 0	--	--	--	103 0
Kalkaska	287 0	7 7	294 7	--	--	--	294 7
Lake	305 6	--	305 6	--	--	--	305 6
Leelanau	114 2	0 4	114 6	25 2	--	25 2	139 8
Manistee	242 1	1 6	243 7	--	--	--	243 7
Mason	172 8	1 7	174 5	3 9	--	3 9	178 4
Mecosta	128 0	2 0	130 0	--	--	--	130 0
Midland	155 8	--	155 8	--	--	--	155 8
Missaukee	226 5	2 5	229 0	--	--	--	229 0
Montmorency	290 0	8 4	298 4	--	--	--	298 4
Newaygo	316 8	--	316 8	--	--	--	316 8
Oceana	174 8	4 3	179 0	--	--	--	179 0
Ogemaw	222 1	--	222 1	2 0	--	2 0	224 2
Osceola	163 1	--	163 1	--	--	--	163 1
Oscoda	296 1	17 5	313 6	1 7	--	1 7	315 3
Otsego	249 6	1 5	251 1	--	--	--	251 1
Presque sle	313 6	4 6	318 2	--	--	--	318 2
Roscommon	266 2	5 6	271 8	--	--	--	271 8
Wexford	259 6	1 5	261 1	--	--	--	261 1
Total	7 164 2	97 8	7 262 0	44 1	--	44 1	7 306 1

(Table 54 continued on next page)

74

(Table 54 continued)

Forest Survey Unit and county	Unreserved forests			Reserved forests			All forest land
	Timberland	Unproductive	Total	Productive	Unproductive	Total	
Southern Lower Peninsula							
Allegan	165 4	--	165 4	2 1	--	2 1	167 6
Barry	115 2	--	115 2	--	--	--	115 2
Berrien	85 4	--	85 4	1 8	--	1 8	87 2
Branch	67 8	--	67 8	--	--	--	67 8
Calhoun	70 2	--	70 2	1 8	--	1 8	72 1
Cass	75 7	--	75 7	--	--	--	75 7
Clinton	35 5	--	35 5	--	--	--	35 5
Eaton	50 6	--	50 6	--	--	--	50 6
Genesee	77 8	--	77 8	--	--	--	77 8
Gratiot	42 0	--	42 0	--	--	--	42 0
Hillsdale	56 2	--	56 2	--	--	--	56 2
Huron	64 3	--	64 3	--	--	--	64 3
ngham	51 9	--	51 9	--	--	--	51 9
onia	63 3	--	63 3	--	--	--	63 3
Jackson	110 5	1 9	112 4	--	--	--	112 4
Kalamazoo	98 4	--	98 4	--	--	--	98 4
Kent	142 3	--	142 3	--	--	--	142 3
Lapeer	117 6	--	117 6	--	--	--	117 6
Lenawee	71 2	--	71 2	--	--	--	71 2
Livingston	85 3	--	85 3	--	--	--	85 3
Macomb	40 9	--	40 9	--	--	--	40 9
Monroe	43 3	--	43 3	--	--	--	43 3
Montcalm	142 6	--	142 6	--	--	--	142 6
Muskegon	176 7	--	176 7	--	--	--	176 7
Oakland	103 3	--	103 3	2 1	--	2 1	105 3
Ottawa	90 1	0 6	90 7	--	--	--	90 7
Saginaw	87 1	--	87 1	--	--	--	87 1
St Clair	92 8	--	92 8	--	--	--	92 8
St Joseph	65 1	--	65 1	0 6	--	0 6	65 7
Sanilac	78 7	--	78 7	--	--	--	78 7
Shiawassee	48 8	--	48 8	--	--	--	48 8
Tuscola	110 2	--	110 2	--	--	--	110 2
Van Buren	121 0	--	121 0	--	--	--	121 0

(Table 54 continued on next page)

75

(Table 54 continued)

Forest Survey Unit and county	Unreserved forests			Reserved forests			All forest land
	Timberland	Unproductive	Total	Productive	Unproductive	Total	
Southern Lower Peninsula							
Washtenaw	100 7	- -	100 7	- -	- -	- -	100 7
Wayne	44 2	- -	44 2	- -	- -	- -	44 2
Total	2 992 3	2 5	2 994 8	8 4	- -	8 4	3 003 2
All counties	18 745 7	238 6	18 984 2	321 3	6 4	327 7	19 311 9

All table cells without observations in the inventory sample are indicated by -- Table value of 0 0 indicates the acres round to less than 0 1 thousand acres Columns and rows may not add to their totals due to rounding

Table 55.—Area of forest land, in thousand acres, by forest inventory unit, county, ownership group, and forest-land status, Michigan, 2004

Forest Survey Unit and county	Forest Service		Other Federal		State and local government		Undifferentiated private		All forest land
	Timber-land	Other forest land	Timber-land	Other forest land	Timber-land	Other forest land	Timber-land	Other forest land	
Eastern Upper Peninsula									
Alger	120 2	4 4	16 9	4 3	109 1	- -	277 5	4 4	535 7
Chippewa	202 2	12 3	- -	- -	221 7	1 3	359 7	8 9	806 0
Delta	213 1	- -	- -	- -	63 4	2 1	315 1	6 2	599 9
Luce	- -	- -	- -	- -	246 8	7 1	230 0	9 7	493 6
Mackinac	132 0	10 0	0 5	- -	198 5	9 0	229 2	4 1	583 3
Menominee	- -	- -	- -	- -	93 9	- -	420 1	1 8	515 8
Schoolcraft	111 3	6 5	29 7	4 0	209 9	3 2	208 0	4 0	576 5
Total	778 8	33 2	47 0	8 3	1 143 3	22 7	2 039 5	39 1	4 111 9
Western Upper Peninsula									
Baraga	38 1	10 5	9 9	- -	73 3	- -	399 0	4 7	535 5
Dickinson	- -	- -	- -	- -	200 6	- -	206 7	- -	407 3
Gogebic	247 1	19 3	- -	- -	61 6	17 4	307 5	2 6	655 7
Houghton	135 4	14 7	- -	- -	49 5	- -	331 1	2 0	532 6
ron	169 9	- -	- -	- -	87 0	- -	401 7	8 5	667 2
Keweenaw	- -	- -	15 4	115 0	5 6	- -	177 9	10 6	324 5
Marquette	13 0	10 7	2 1	- -	264 3	4 7	713 6	18 8	1 027 2
Ontonagon	250 7	13 9	- -	- -	23 6	52 9	395 8	4 0	740 9
Total	854 3	69 2	27 5	115 0	765 5	75 0	2 933 2	51 1	4 890 7

(Table 55 continued on next page)

(Table 55 continued)

Forest Survey Unit and county	Forest Service		Other Federal		State and local government		Undifferentiated private		All forest land
	Timber-land	Other forest land	Timber-land	Other forest land	Timber-land	Other forest land	Timber-land	Other forest land	
Northern Lower Peninsula									
Alcona	107 1	--	19	--	91	10	199 2	21	320 4
Alpena	--	--	--	--	500	--	2110	43	265 3
Antrim	--	--	--	--	439	--	139 1	--	183 1
Arenac	--	--	--	--	227	20	808	--	105 5
Bay	--	--	--	--	31	--	321	--	35 2
Benzie	--	--	20	58	652	--	656	--	138 7
Charlevoix	--	--	--	--	529	--	1208	--	173 7
Cheboygan	--	--	--	--	1620	58	2008	--	368 6
Clare	--	--	21	--	454	--	1434	01	190 9
Crawford	33 1	58	20	--	1615	52	946	--	302 2
Emmet	--	--	--	--	761	20	1396	--	217 8
Gladwin	--	--	--	--	855	20	1069	--	194 4
Grand Traverse	--	--	--	--	660	33	1011	41	174 6
Iosco	108 6	39	19	--	201	20	1201	--	256 6
Isabella	--	--	--	--	42	--	988	--	103 0
Kalkaska	--	--	38	--	1590	56	1242	21	294 7
Lake	95 3	--	--	--	571	--	1533	--	305 6
Leelanau	--	--	178	231	120	--	844	25	139 8
Manistee	716	16	--	--	241	20	1464	--	243 7
Mason	612	37	--	--	105	20	1011	--	178 4
Mecosta	--	--	--	--	153	20	1126	--	130 0
Midland	--	--	--	--	403	--	1155	--	155 8
Missaukee	--	--	--	--	1011	25	1254	--	229 0
Montmorency	--	--	--	--	1310	19	1590	65	298 4
Newaygo	104 0	--	19	--	82	--	2027	--	316 8
Oceana	44 5	--	--	--	107	--	1196	43	179 0
Ogemaw	19 1	--	31	--	755	20	1245	--	224 2
Osceola	--	--	--	--	238	--	1394	--	163 1
Oscoda	136 1	13 2	--	--	544	20	1056	40	315 3
Otsego	--	--	--	--	862	05	1634	10	251 1
Presque Isle	--	--	--	--	900	19	2236	27	318 2
Roscommon	--	--	--	--	1798	56	864	--	271 8
Wexford	88 5	--	--	--	540	15	1171	--	261 1
Total	869 2	28 2	367	28 9	2 000 5	50 9	4 257 9	33 9	7 306 1

(Table 55 continued on next page)

78

(Table 55 continued)

Forest Survey Unit and county	Forest Service		Other Federal		State and local government		Undifferentiated private		All forest land
	Timber-land	Other forest land	Timber-land	Other forest land	Timber-land	Other forest land	Timber-land	Other forest land	
Southern Lower Peninsula									
Allegan	--	--	2 0	--	457	2 1	1177	--	167 6
Barry	--	--	--	--	224	--	928	--	115 2
Berrien	--	--	--	--	73	--	781	1 8	87 2
Branch	--	--	--	--	24	--	654	--	67 8
Calhoun	--	--	2 2	--	51	1 8	629	--	72 1
Cass	--	--	--	--	36	--	721	--	75 7
Clinton	--	--	--	--	39	--	316	--	35 5
Eaton	--	--	--	--	79	--	427	--	50 6
Genesee	--	--	--	--	133	--	644	--	77 8
Gratiot	--	--	--	--	101	--	319	--	42 0
Hillsdale	--	--	--	--	15	--	547	--	56 2
Huron	--	--	--	--	158	--	485	--	64 3
ngham	--	--	--	--	78	--	442	--	51 9
onia	--	--	--	--	86	--	547	--	63 3
Jackson	--	--	--	--	119	--	987	1 9	112 4
Kalamazoo	--	--	2 2	--	105	--	857	--	98 4
Kent	--	--	--	--	170	--	1252	--	142 3
Lapeer	--	--	--	--	171	--	1005	--	117 6
Lenawee	--	--	--	--	34	--	678	--	71 2
Livingston	--	--	--	--	127	--	726	--	85 3
Macomb	--	--	--	--	88	--	321	--	40 9
Monroe	--	--	--	--	24	--	409	--	43 3
Montcalm	--	--	1 9	--	276	--	1131	--	142 6
Muskegon	9 4	--	1 7	--	376	--	1280	--	176 7
Oakland	--	--	--	--	193	2 1	839	--	105 3
Ottawa	--	--	--	--	64	0 6	837	--	90 7
Saginaw	--	--	--	--	79	--	793	--	87 1
St Clair	--	--	--	--	123	--	806	--	92 8
St Joseph	--	--	--	--	64	--	587	0 6	65 7
Sanilac	--	--	--	--	75	--	713	--	78 7
Shiawassee	--	--	--	--	31	--	457	--	48 8
Tuscola	--	--	--	--	277	--	825	--	110 2
Van Buren	--	--	--	--	90	--	1120	--	121 0

(Table 55 continued on next page)

79

(Table 55 continued)

Forest Survey Unit and county	Forest Service		Other Federal		State and local government		Undifferentiated private		All forest land
	Timber-land	Other forest land	Timber-land	Other forest land	Timber-land	Other forest land	Timber-land	Other forest land	
Southern Lower Peninsula									
Washtenaw	--	--	--	--	21 9	--	78 8	--	100 7
Wayne	--	--	--	--	13 5	--	30 7	--	44 2
Total	9 4	--	101	--	439 2	6 6	2 533 6	4 2	3 003 2
All counties	2 511 6	130 5	121 3	152 2	4 348 5	155 2	11 764 3	128 3	19 311 9

All table cells without observations in the inventory sample are indicated by -- Table value of 0 0 indicates the acres round to less than 0 1 thousand acres Columns and rows may not add to their totals due to rounding

Table 56.—Area of forest land, in thousand acres, by forest inventory unit, county, and forest-type group, Michigan, 2004

Forest Survey Unit and county	White-red-jack pine	Spruce-fir	Pinyon-juniper	Douglas-fir	Fir-spruce-mt. hemlock	Exotic softwoods	Oak-pine	Oak-hickory	Oak-gum-cypress	Elm-ash-cottonwood	Maple-beech-birch	Aspen-birch	Exotic hardwoods	Non-stocked	All groups
Eastern Upper Peninsula															
Alger	71.3	73.1	--	--	--	--	7.8	--	1.8	21.5	331.1	25.9	--	4.2	536.7
Chippewa	125.6	243.8	--	--	--	2.2	12.3	7.2	--	38.6	191.3	177.5	--	7.5	806.0
Delta	80.9	202.4	--	--	--	1.3	4.4	6.9	--	33.8	133.8	131.7	--	4.7	599.9
Luce	99.7	148.6	--	--	--	2.4	13.3	3.3	2.1	8.9	176.5	32.4	--	6.4	493.6
Mackinac	31.3	214.9	--	--	--	--	4.0	--	--	14.7	162.2	149.6	--	6.4	583.3
Menominee	13.8	174.6	--	--	--	7.3	5.7	11.7	--	50.8	148.8	102.7	--	0.6	515.8
Schoolcraft	122.7	166.0	--	--	--	--	13.2	3.4	--	23.4	134.7	106.8	--	6.4	576.5
Total	545.3	1,223.4	--	--	--	13.2	60.7	32.5	4.0	191.7	1,278.4	726.5	--	36.2	4,111.9
Western Upper Peninsula															
Baraga	36.2	93.5	--	--	--	--	7.2	4.9	--	21.6	332.2	39.8	--	--	535.5
Dickinson	14.6	118.5	--	--	1.3	--	4.4	6.0	--	10.4	129.8	120.0	--	2.3	407.3
Gogebic	38.5	82.4	--	--	--	1.7	--	4.1	--	39.4	412.5	76.0	--	1.0	655.7
Houghton	35.0	51.5	--	--	--	1.0	6.8	8.2	--	10.5	357.8	57.3	--	4.5	532.6
Iron	35.4	119.0	--	--	--	--	17.2	5.6	--	9.5	303.8	170.7	--	6.1	667.2
Keweenaw	7.4	78.3	--	--	--	--	2.0	3.5	--	6.8	141.8	84.2	--	0.5	324.5
Marquette	122.2	227.5	--	--	--	--	19.5	16.1	--	23.9	458.7	155.5	--	3.7	1,027.2
Ontonagon	30.3	41.6	--	--	--	2.1	2.3	1.5	--	28.2	442.8	187.2	--	4.8	740.9
Total	319.7	812.3	--	--	1.3	4.9	59.4	49.9	--	150.3	2,579.4	890.8	--	22.8	4,890.7

(Table 56 continued on next page)

(Table 56 continued)

Forest Survey Unit and county	White-red-jack pine	Spruce-fir	Pinyon-juniper	Douglas-fir	Fir-spruce-mt. hemlock	Exotic softwoods	Oak-pine	Oak-hickory	Oak-gum-cypress	Elm-ash-cottonwood	Maple-beech-birch	Aspen-birch	Exotic hardwoods	Non-stocked	All groups
Northern Lower Peninsula															
Alcona	34.3	24.5	--	--	--	2.0	11.9	64.8	--	12.6	80.3	88.7	--	1.3	320.4
Alpena	17.2	47.2	--	--	--	4.6	5.7	14.9	--	43.5	45.8	84.4	--	2.0	265.3
Antrim	10.9	5.9	--	--	--	3.7	1.6	--	--	9.3	127.3	21.1	--	3.3	183.1
Arenac	6.9	--	--	--	--	--	7.7	23.0	--	20.9	28.7	16.1	--	2.1	105.5
Bay	--	--	--	--	--	--	--	6.7	--	6.9	6.0	15.6	--	--	35.2
Benzie	16.5	4.5	--	--	--	2.3	2.9	--	--	8.2	94.9	7.3	--	2.1	138.7
Charlevoix	7.1	24.8	--	--	--	--	1.5	4.1	--	4.4	107.5	23.7	--	0.6	173.7
Cheboygan	32.5	61.6	--	--	--	6.3	19.3	15.7	2.0	14.1	96.3	118.5	--	2.3	368.6
Clare	19.1	6.2	--	--	1.3	--	9.1	61.2	--	20.6	31.9	40.9	--	0.7	190.9
Crawford	100.1	22.1	--	--	--	--	36.7	77.6	--	--	23.3	41.9	--	0.5	302.2
Emmet	5.1	28.2	--	1.6	--	3.2	--	4.1	--	6.2	112.4	54.8	--	2.1	217.8
Gladwin	11.4	1.7	--	--	--	--	4.6	40.1	--	32.6	26.6	71.8	--	5.7	194.4
Grand Traverse	25.9	13.5	--	--	--	0.2	17.8	37.1	2.1	13.7	48.8	15.4	--	--	174.6
osco	96.6	24.3	--	--	--	0.5	18.1	27.8	--	19.4	32.7	36.1	--	1.0	256.6
sabella	7.5	2.2	--	--	--	2.1	1.1	22.6	--	19.9	21.8	24.1	--	1.7	103.0
Kalkaska	80.3	25.9	--	--	--	5.3	12.3	21.1	1.2	6.0	101.3	34.7	--	6.6	294.7
Lake	81.3	7.2	--	--	1.1	4.3	24.8	113.5	--	9.9	29.5	34.1	--	--	305.6
Leelanau	10.9	10.3	2.1	--	1.6	--	1.6	6.2	--	6.5	88.0	10.3	--	2.3	139.8
Manistee	30.7	4.3	--	--	2.1	2.7	16.6	67.4	--	11.2	83.4	20.6	--	4.8	243.7
Mason	31.8	2.4	--	--	1.8	5.2	11.8	53.4	2.1	27.5	19.1	18.9	--	4.4	178.4
Mecosta	14.5	--	--	--	--	4.8	1.6	27.7	2.1	18.5	25.6	34.0	--	1.1	130.0
Midland	2.1	--	--	--	--	--	6.7	57.6	4.2	22.7	28.1	32.8	--	1.6	155.8
Missaukee	30.1	18.1	--	--	--	7.8	9.7	27.2	--	15.7	53.4	65.9	--	1.1	229.0
Montmorency	44.2	29.1	--	--	--	--	19.9	54.0	--	5.1	68.4	77.1	--	0.5	298.4
Newaygo	47.7	5.7	--	--	--	8.4	12.9	139.1	--	27.2	45.6	29.7	--	0.5	316.8
Oceana	25.4	4.6	--	--	0.9	5.1	7.3	53.7	--	21.4	42.7	17.9	--	--	179.0
Ogemaw	47.5	13.1	--	--	--	0.5	7.2	41.1	--	26.3	28.1	58.2	--	2.0	224.2
Osceola	13.7	--	--	--	--	5.5	2.8	23.6	--	12.3	55.4	49.9	--	--	163.1
Oscoda	98.8	17.8	--	--	--	--	36.5	52.6	--	2.7	24.9	82.0	--	--	315.3
Otsego	48.2	14.1	--	--	1.3	2.1	20.1	7.4	1.1	--	107.8	48.1	--	1.0	251.1
Presque Isle	28.9	65.8	--	--	--	--	5.5	27.9	--	25.2	57.6	104.7	--	2.5	318.2
Roscommon	29.2	32.3	--	--	--	--	18.0	82.2	--	17.1	31.2	58.2	--	3.5	271.8
Wexford	53.2	12.0	--	--	1.9	14.5	8.1	21.6	--	6.1	103.1	37.1	--	3.4	261.1
Total	1,109.9	529.6	2.1	2.5	11.0	91.2	361.3	1,276.6	14.9	493.8	1,877.4	1,474.8	--	60.7	7,306.1

(Table 56 continued on next page)

82

(Table 56 continued)

| | Forest type group | | | | | | | | | | | | | | |
Forest Survey Unit and county	White-red-jack pine	Spruce-fir	Pinyon-juniper	Douglas-fir	Fir-spruce-mt hemlock	Exotic softwoods	Oak-pine	Oak-hickory	Oak-gum-cypress	Elm-ash-cottonwood	Maple-beech-birch	Aspen-birch	Exotic hardwoods	Non-stocked	All groups
Southern Lower Peninsula															
Allegan	7.5	--	--	--	--	5.3	6.7	85.4	6.4	22.2	28.1	4.0	--	2.0	167.6
Barry	1.0	4.4	--	2.1	--	1.1	--	54.6	--	20.7	27.7	3.1	--	0.6	115.2
Berrien	--	--	--	--	--	2.0	--	32.6	6.3	15.9	29.8	--	--	0.6	87.2
Branch	--	--	--	--	--	--	--	25.0	--	28.9	13.9	--	--	--	67.8
Calhoun	2.2	--	--	--	--	--	--	25.8	--	23.7	18.9	1.4	--	--	72.1
Cass	1.9	--	--	--	--	0.9	--	33.5	--	19.1	19.9	--	--	0.5	75.7
Clinton	--	--	--	--	--	--	--	11.4	--	11.4	12.0	--	--	0.7	35.5
Eaton	--	--	--	--	--	0.2	--	16.1	4.6	10.2	19.4	--	--	--	50.6
Genesee	--	--	--	--	--	--	--	28.1	--	20.4	18.9	9.3	--	1.0	77.8
Gratiot	4.1	--	--	--	--	--	--	3.7	--	19.4	13.7	1.0	--	--	42.0
Hillsdale	1.4	--	--	--	--	1.8	--	29.5	--	9.2	14.3	--	--	--	56.2
Huron	--	--	--	--	--	0.6	1.8	10.9	--	16.2	27.0	7.8	--	--	64.3
ngham	--	0.4	--	--	--	1.5	--	18.4	--	11.1	18.9	1.6	--	--	51.9
onia	1.3	--	--	--	--	2.0	2.4	19.1	--	11.3	23.5	1.1	2.1	0.5	63.3
Jackson	1.9	--	1.1	--	--	2.0	--	65.9	--	13.5	18.9	5.1	0.6	3.3	112.4
Kalamazoo	4.3	--	--	--	--	3.2	2.2	40.9	--	16.0	29.1	--	--	2.7	98.4
Kent	2.4	4.1	--	--	--	5.4	2.4	55.2	--	25.8	34.5	10.1	--	2.4	142.3
Lapeer	2.3	1.2	--	--	--	3.2	4.1	37.2	1.8	30.9	30.3	5.9	--	0.6	117.6
Lenawee	--	--	--	--	--	--	1.8	33.3	--	18.4	17.7	--	--	--	71.2
Livingston	--	--	--	--	1.2	--	--	44.1	--	24.0	10.2	0.2	1.8	3.8	85.3
Macomb	--	--	--	--	--	--	2.4	8.6	--	8.9	19.5	--	--	1.5	40.9
Monroe	--	--	--	--	--	--	2.4	18.6	--	19.7	2.6	--	--	--	43.3
Montcalm	4.5	2.4	--	--	--	2.6	6.2	57.5	4.0	23.3	28.2	13.9	--	--	142.6
Muskegon	20.8	0.3	--	--	--	4.6	13.2	103.6	--	16.3	13.9	3.5	--	0.5	176.7
Oakland	0.6	--	--	--	--	1.2	1.2	56.4	1.7	18.2	19.8	5.5	--	2.0	105.3
Ottawa	11.9	--	--	--	--	3.4	2.4	25.1	3.7	12.7	27.5	3.4	--	0.6	90.7
Saginaw	3.2	--	--	--	--	2.3	0.1	53.0	--	18.1	8.9	0.8	--	0.9	87.1
St. Clair	1.1	--	--	--	--	--	1.5	30.5	1.8	20.4	31.3	5.7	--	0.6	92.8
St. Joseph	1.2	--	--	--	--	--	1.1	32.8	1.1	13.0	9.9	--	2.4	4.1	65.7
Sanilac	--	--	--	--	--	--	1.8	13.8	--	22.4	25.0	14.1	--	1.6	78.7
Shiawassee	--	0.6	--	--	--	--	1.0	16.8	1.0	15.3	13.3	--	--	1.8	48.8
Tuscola	1.1	1.4	--	--	--	5.2	3.0	20.7	1.3	29.9	31.7	15.3	--	0.5	110.2
Van Buren	4.0	0.5	--	--	--	1.5	--	57.9	3.9	16.2	33.0	3.0	--	0.9	121.0
Washtenaw	2.3	--	--	--	--	0.7	1.5	51.2	--	18.0	22.8	1.5	--	2.7	100.7
Wayne	--	--	--	--	--	--	--	15.0	--	16.0	13.2	--	--	--	44.2
Total	80.9	15.3	1.1	2.1	1.2	49.6	58.4	1,232.1	37.7	636.7	727.3	117.5	6.9	36.3	3,003.2
All counties	2,055.8	2,580.7	3.3	4.5	13.6	158.9	539.9	2,591.1	56.6	1,472.5	6,462.5	3,209.6	6.9	156.1	19,311.9

All table cells without observations in the inventory sample are indicated by --. Table value of 0.0 indicates the acres round to less than 0.1 thousand acres. Columns and rows may not add to their totals due to rounding.

83

Table 57.—Area of timberland, in thousand acres, by forest inventory unit, county, and stand-size class, Michigan, 2004

Forest Survey Unit and county	Large diameter	Medium diameter	Stand-size class Small diameter	Chaparral	Nonstocked	All size classes
Eastern Upper Peninsula						
Alger	272.7	184.3	62.6	- -	4.2	523.7
Chippewa	249.1	336.1	193.0	- -	5.4	783.6
Delta	202.8	211.4	172.7	- -	4.7	591.6
Luce	197.0	175.3	98.6	- -	5.9	476.8
Mackinac	204.5	229.0	120.4	- -	6.4	560.2
Menominee	121.2	266.6	125.6	- -	0.6	514.0
Schoolcraft	174.6	197.1	180.8	- -	6.4	558.8
Total	1 421.8	1 599.8	953.6	- -	33.5	4 008.6
Western Upper Peninsula						
Baraga	249.0	191.6	79.7	- -	- -	520.3
Dickinson	122.1	187.4	95.5	- -	2.3	407.3
Gogebic	244.7	306.4	64.1	- -	1.0	616.3
Houghton	264.5	184.6	62.3	- -	4.5	515.9
ron	242.7	279.7	130.2	- -	6.1	658.7
Keweenaw	113.0	62.2	23.7	- -	- -	198.9
Marquette	334.7	447.0	207.7	- -	3.7	993.0
Ontonagon	231.3	324.7	109.3	- -	4.8	670.1
Total	1 802.0	1 983.7	772.5	- -	22.3	4 580.5

(Table 57 continued on next page)

(Table 57 continued)

Forest Survey Unit and county	Stand-size class					All size classes
	Large diameter	Medium diameter	Small diameter	Chaparral	Nonstocked	
Northern Lower Peninsula						
Alcona	111 9	158 9	45 3	- -	1 3	317 3
Alpena	73 5	114 9	70 6	- -	2 0	261 0
Antrim	71 0	95 8	13 0	- -	3 3	183 1
Arenac	35 1	55 4	10 8	- -	2 1	103 5
Bay	13 4	17 7	4 1	- -	- -	35 2
Benzie	55 9	51 5	23 3	- -	2 1	132 8
Charlevoix	90 4	67 0	15 7	- -	0 6	173 7
Cheboygan	123 4	149 9	87 2	- -	2 3	362 7
Clare	75 9	70 2	44 1	- -	0 7	190 9
Crawford	92 4	116 1	82 2	- -	0 5	291 2
Emmet	90 4	93 5	29 6	- -	2 1	215 7
Gladwin	71 1	60 4	55 2	- -	5 7	192 4
Grand Traverse	65 8	72 5	28 8	- -	- -	167 1
osco	97 6	109 2	42 9	- -	1 0	250 7
sabella	38 7	38 9	23 7	- -	1 7	103 0
Kalkaska	84 6	135 9	59 9	- -	6 6	287 0
Lake	148 5	103 8	53 3	- -	- -	305 6
Leelanau	64 7	30 3	16 9	- -	2 3	114 2
Manistee	116 7	83 2	37 3	- -	4 8	242 1
Mason	83 0	62 8	23 9	- -	3 0	172 8
Mecosta	52 4	52 8	22 2	- -	0 5	128 0
Midland	49 8	69 2	35 2	- -	1 6	155 8
Missaukee	66 8	113 8	44 8	- -	1 1	226 5
Montmorency	101 6	118 3	69 6	- -	0 5	290 0
Newaygo	180 8	99 3	36 2	- -	0 5	316 8
Oceana	80 6	69 2	24 9	- -	- -	174 8
Ogemaw	52 5	97 8	69 7	- -	2 0	222 1
Osceola	67 8	65 1	30 2	- -	- -	163 1
Oscoda	86 0	117 8	92 3	- -	- -	296 1
Otsego	89 0	124 7	34 9	- -	1 0	249 6
Presque sle	68 7	146 9	95 5	- -	2 5	313 6
Roscommon	78 1	97 8	86 7	- -	3 5	266 2
Wexford	111 8	99 9	44 5	- -	3 4	259 6
Total	2 689 7	2 960 8	1 455 0	- -	58 8	7 164 2

(Table 57 continued on next page)

85

(Table 57 continued)

Forest Survey Unit and county	Stand-size class					All size classes
	Large diameter	Medium diameter	Small diameter	Chaparral	Nonstocked	
Southern Lower Peninsula						
Allegan	88 3	50 4	24 7	--	2 0	165 4
Barry	63 3	33 8	17 5	--	0 6	115 2
Berrien	62 5	15 1	7 2	--	0 6	85 4
Branch	47 5	15 0	5 2	--	--	67 8
Calhoun	51 7	11 7	6 8	--	--	70 2
Cass	45 6	16 0	13 6	--	0 5	75 7
Clinton	18 6	11 1	5 1	--	0 7	35 5
Eaton	27 9	16 4	6 4	--	--	50 6
Genesee	42 0	25 0	9 7	--	1 0	77 8
Gratiot	18 0	19 0	5 1	--	--	42 0
Hillsdale	34 2	19 6	2 4	--	--	56 2
Huron	24 6	30 4	9 3	--	--	64 3
ngham	25 2	20 1	6 6	--	--	51 9
onia	30 8	23 0	9 0	--	0 5	63 3
Jackson	72 2	17 5	17 5	--	3 3	110 5
Kalamazoo	57 6	25 5	12 5	--	2 7	98 4
Kent	69 1	48 5	22 3	--	2 4	142 3
Lapeer	59 4	38 8	18 9	--	0 6	117 6
Lenawee	42 5	20 7	8 1	--	--	71 2
Livingston	43 3	26 8	11 4	--	3 8	85 3
Macomb	20 5	14 8	4 2	--	1 5	40 9
Monroe	30 5	7 6	5 2	--	--	43 3
Montcalm	61 7	56 7	24 2	--	--	142 6
Muskegon	105 3	50 2	20 6	--	0 5	176 7
Oakland	55 3	32 0	14 1	--	2 0	103 3
Ottawa	51 5	27 2	11 3	--	--	90 1
Saginaw	43 1	38 8	4 4	--	0 9	87 1
St Clair	40 8	31 6	19 8	--	0 6	92 8
St Joseph	48 8	10 9	1 3	--	4 1	65 1
Sanilac	21 7	38 5	16 9	--	1 6	78 7
Shiawassee	21 0	9 9	16 2	--	1 8	48 8
Tuscola	29 9	59 8	20 0	--	0 5	110 2
Van Buren	69 6	35 2	15 4	--	0 9	121 0

(Table 57 continued on next page)

(Table 57 continued)

Forest Survey Unit and county	Stand-size class					
	Large diameter	Medium diameter	Small diameter	Chaparral	Nonstocked	All size classes
Southern Lower Peninsula						
Washtenaw	44 1	31 9	22 0	- -	2 7	100 7
Wayne	22 5	11 8	9 8	- -	- -	44 2
Total	1 590 6	941 3	424 7	- -	35 7	2 992 3
All counties	7 504 1	7 485 6	3 605 7	- -	150 3	18 745 7

All table cells without observations in the inventory sample are indicated by -- Table value of 0 0 indicates the acres round to less than 0 1 thousand acres Columns and rows may not add to their totals due to rounding

Table 58.—Area of timberland, in thousand acres, by forest inventory unit, county, and stocking class, Michigan, 2004

| Forest Survey Unit and county | Stocking class of growing-stock trees | | | | | |
	Nonstocked	Poorly stocked	Moderately stocked	Fully stocked	Over-stocked	All classes
Eastern Upper Peninsula						
Alger	4 7	43 5	147 2	277 0	51 4	523 7
Chippewa	11 9	76 3	302 7	340 6	52 2	783 6
Delta	6 7	60 1	220 0	240 4	64 4	591 6
Luce	6 0	42 2	167 6	239 4	21 5	476 8
Mackinac	7 0	47 4	151 5	299 1	55 2	560 2
Menominee	4 0	55 7	146 4	262 0	45 9	514 0
Schoolcraft	11 3	94 7	204 9	205 0	43 0	558 8
Total	51 4	419 9	1 340 2	1 863 6	333 5	4 008 6
Western Upper Peninsula						
Baraga	- -	23 3	132 1	313 2	51 7	520 3
Dickinson	2 9	43 7	117 1	186 8	56 7	407 3
Gogebic	3 1	31 1	174 2	339 8	68 1	616 3
Houghton	4 7	27 5	131 0	294 3	58 5	515 9
ron	6 7	57 6	196 7	355 5	42 1	658 7
Keweenaw	- -	13 2	52 4	128 8	4 5	198 9
Marquette	6 7	95 2	258 7	512 7	119 8	993 0
Ontonagon	10 0	37 2	188 2	356 0	78 6	670 1
Total	34 2	328 7	1 250 5	2 487 1	479 9	4 580 5

(Table 58 continued on next page)

88

(Table 58 continued)

Forest Survey Unit and county	Stocking class of growing-stock trees					
	Nonstocked	Poorly stocked	Moderately stocked	Fully stocked	Over-stocked	All classes
Northern Lower Peninsula						
Alcona	1 3	37 6	118 7	144 4	15 2	317 3
Alpena	3 5	28 8	119 9	98 8	9 9	261 0
Antrim	8 3	17 8	46 5	95 7	14 7	183 1
Arenac	2 5	17 5	34 2	46 5	2 8	103 5
Bay	0 6	2 1	16 8	14 8	0 8	35 2
Benzie	2 2	14 0	34 0	64 9	17 7	132 8
Charlevoix	1 6	17 7	50 1	81 8	22 4	173 7
Cheboygan	7 2	27 3	101 0	192 7	34 5	362 7
Clare	3 5	19 1	64 7	85 4	18 2	190 9
Crawford	5 4	44 3	91 5	114 5	35 5	291 2
Emmet	2 2	19 3	51 2	115 4	27 8	215 7
Gladwin	5 8	46 0	65 5	55 9	19 1	192 4
Grand Traverse	0 8	23 8	60 0	71 4	11 2	167 1
osco	1 5	25 7	110 9	98 0	14 6	250 7
sabella	3 9	14 4	39 5	35 0	10 3	103 0
Kalkaska	14 1	39 1	71 5	137 6	24 7	287 0
Lake	0 6	54 7	108 0	121 1	21 3	305 6
Leelanau	4 6	8 2	32 1	46 8	22 6	114 2
Manistee	7 1	31 9	67 5	115 2	20 4	242 1
Mason	5 0	20 5	55 1	83 6	8 5	172 8
Mecosta	7 7	16 3	52 6	49 5	1 8	128 0
Midland	1 9	16 6	66 6	61 8	8 9	155 8
Missaukee	3 0	37 2	73 1	96 1	17 1	226 5
Montmorency	3 7	39 8	91 9	139 6	15 0	290 0
Newaygo	5 2	56 2	97 1	144 7	13 5	316 8
Oceana	3 1	15 7	71 5	73 5	10 9	174 8
Ogemaw	2 5	30 6	57 2	95 3	36 6	222 1
Osceola	3 1	25 1	60 6	62 1	12 2	163 1
Oscoda	1 4	36 7	97 5	123 2	37 3	296 1
Otsego	5 6	40 4	82 7	95 6	25 3	249 6
Presque sle	3 9	47 8	78 3	131 3	52 2	313 6
Roscommon	6 7	37 1	86 3	104 5	31 5	266 2
Wexford	4 4	36 4	66 8	132 9	19 1	259 6
Total	134 0	945 8	2 320 8	3 129 6	634 0	7 164 2

(Table 58 continued on next page)

89

(Table 58 continued)

Forest Survey Unit and county	Stocking class of growing-stock trees					All classes
	Nonstocked	Poorly stocked	Moderately stocked	Fully stocked	Over-stocked	
Southern Lower Peninsula						
Allegan	3 9	38 7	60 4	49 0	13 5	165 4
Barry	1 6	33 9	44 3	29 4	5 9	115 2
Berrien	3 8	19 1	34 6	26 9	0 9	85 4
Branch	--	22 2	22 2	23 4	--	67 8
Calhoun	0 8	13 6	33 1	21 0	1 8	70 2
Cass	1 1	29 4	26 7	17 7	0 8	75 7
Clinton	1 1	9 9	16 4	6 4	1 7	35 5
Eaton	--	6 3	19 7	22 4	2 3	50 6
Genesee	1 0	24 9	26 3	25 1	0 4	77 8
Gratiot	0 0	10 2	14 3	15 3	2 2	42 0
Hillsdale	0 3	18 3	25 6	10 4	1 5	56 2
Huron	--	17 0	14 8	26 1	6 4	64 3
ngham	2 0	13 9	20 3	15 8	--	51 9
onia	6 5	14 3	18 7	21 4	2 4	63 3
Jackson	8 2	24 0	34 6	43 2	0 5	110 5
Kalamazoo	6 6	11 8	30 8	41 5	7 6	98 4
Kent	5 0	24 3	68 4	41 2	3 4	142 3
Lapeer	0 7	32 3	49 2	27 7	7 7	117 6
Lenawee	4 9	12 2	30 2	22 8	1 1	71 2
Livingston	8 0	16 6	40 1	18 4	2 1	85 3
Macomb	1 5	7 3	21 4	10 7	--	40 9
Monroe	0 2	7 7	17 4	17 4	0 6	43 3
Montcalm	4 1	38 1	46 5	52 6	1 3	142 6
Muskegon	3 6	20 2	61 9	87 9	3 1	176 7
Oakland	8 7	24 1	32 8	36 4	1 3	103 3
Ottawa	0 9	14 7	33 9	34 9	5 8	90 1
Saginaw	1 6	4 6	40 5	37 2	3 2	87 1
St Clair	0 8	13 9	37 2	38 2	2 8	92 8
St Joseph	5 6	9 5	26 7	21 8	1 4	65 1
Sanilac	1 8	20 7	30 0	24 6	1 6	78 7
Shiawassee	4 6	9 1	21 1	12 3	1 8	48 8
Tuscola	1 1	21 9	39 2	44 9	3 2	110 2
Van Buren	2 0	25 1	51 3	40 1	2 6	121 0

(Table 58 continued on next page)

(Table 58 continued)

		Stocking class of growing-stock trees				
Forest Survey Unit and county	Nonstocked	Poorly stocked	Moderately stocked	Fully stocked	Over-stocked	All classes
Southern Lower Peninsula						
Washtenaw	4 7	32 9	37 3	21 5	4 3	100 7
Wayne	3 4	10 7	9 4	20 2	0 5	44 2
Total	100 3	653 3	1 137 1	1 006 1	95 5	2 992 3
All counties	320 0	2 347 7	6 048 6	8 486 4	1 543 0	18 745 7

All table cells without observations in the inventory sample are indicated by -- Table value of 0 0 indicates the acres round to less than 0 1 thousand acres Columns and rows may not add to their totals due to rounding

91

Table 59.—Net volume of growing-stock trees (at least 5 inches d.b.h.), in million cubic feet, and sawtimber trees, in million board feet (International ¼-inch rule), on timberland by forest inventory unit, county, and major species group, Michigan, 2004

Forest Survey Unit and county	Growing stock					Sawtimber				
	Major species group					Major species group				
	Pine	Other softwoods	Soft hardwoods	Hard hardwoods	All species	Pine	Other softwoods	Soft hardwoods	Hard hardwoods	All species
Eastern Upper Peninsula										
Alger	81.2	233.1	238.7	344.2	897.2	370.7	899.1	541.5	966.7	2 777.9
Chippewa	168.0	367.1	316.4	179.4	1 030.9	677.6	1 012.7	710.9	457.9	2 859.2
Delta	113.7	308.0	237.0	104.1	762.8	467.1	806.5	506.2	295.1	2 075.0
Luce	136.3	212.4	168.5	147.1	664.4	592.8	661.6	384.7	416.1	2 055.3
Mackinac	64.2	363.8	233.5	166.4	827.9	290.5	938.7	539.8	487.6	2 256.6
Menominee	45.2	273.7	199.1	146.1	664.2	215.5	632.3	384.2	346.4	1 578.4
Schoolcraft	154.4	203.0	172.8	92.8	623.0	603.5	525.9	373.1	275.4	1 777.9
Total	763.1	1 961.1	1 566.1	1 180.2	5 470.4	3 217.7	5 476.9	3 440.3	3 245.2	15 380.2
Western Upper Peninsula										
Baraga	33.7	230.5	256.4	365.9	886.5	134.4	869.3	596.6	1 003.8	2 604.1
Dickinson	36.7	197.7	195.3	136.1	565.8	176.6	504.3	473.6	276.0	1 430.5
Gogebic	55.0	244.4	345.7	445.9	1 091.0	252.3	882.5	829.5	1 049.8	3 014.1
Houghton	61.4	217.1	299.9	365.5	943.9	291.5	878.7	728.2	1 023.9	2 922.3
Iron	89.5	211.6	289.3	364.5	954.8	420.1	632.0	622.3	961.9	2 636.4
Keweenaw	26.8	117.0	91.7	123.2	358.8	139.6	441.1	230.4	368.0	1 179.0
Marquette	163.8	459.3	445.4	424.2	1 492.7	737.3	1 451.4	933.8	1 130.7	4 253.1
Ontonagon	50.6	217.4	424.6	374.1	1 066.8	256.9	868.1	958.4	930.5	3 013.8
Total	517.5	1 895.2	2 348.1	2 599.4	7 360.3	2 408.7	6 527.4	5 372.8	6 744.5	21 053.4

(Table 59 continued on next page)

(Table 59 continued)

	Growing stock					Sawtimber				
	Major species group					Major species group				
Forest Survey Unit and county	Pine	Other softwoods	Soft hardwoods	Hard hardwoods	All species	Pine	Other softwoods	Soft hardwoods	Hard hardwoods	All species
Northern Lower Peninsula										
Alcona	81 8	50 7	178 1	155 6	466 2	309 2	152 0	340 8	452 2	1 254 1
Alpena	51 9	77 8	126 3	59 5	315 5	231 3	192 1	245 2	171 9	840 5
Antrim	25 5	19 8	101 6	151 6	298 4	76 4	65 5	262 4	329 9	734 2
Arenac	14 2	3 8	79 0	40 4	137 5	53 9	11 9	187 0	115 5	368 2
Bay	1 7	1 3	39 9	13 8	56 7	8 9	4 0	101 7	46 2	160 8
Benzie	31 3	12 4	77 7	104 8	226 3	81 3	29 3	204 0	308 2	622 7
Charlevoix	28 5	69 2	96 3	131 0	324 9	138 8	207 5	273 4	346 3	966 0
Cheboygan	85 6	109 6	196 0	102 8	494 0	330 3	286 4	429 4	245 5	1 291 6
Clare	42 8	18 4	140 1	72 9	274 3	168 1	55 3	294 6	246 6	764 6
Crawford	119 3	20 7	59 5	96 8	296 3	424 1	40 0	100 2	254 0	818 3
Emmet	25 6	45 0	112 6	160 7	344 0	98 6	115 1	313 1	406 6	933 4
Gladwin	24 2	4 6	142 1	34 4	205 3	77 7	7 6	380 3	105 5	571 1
Grand Traverse	75 2	33 9	59 1	84 7	252 9	208 6	94 0	128 4	262 9	693 9
Iosco	157 3	46 1	114 5	57 9	375 8	579 1	109 0	311 6	155 4	1 155 1
Isabella	13 7	6 4	73 7	43 4	137 1	44 7	16 6	204 7	135 5	401 4
Kalkaska	154 3	26 6	109 2	102 4	392 5	475 2	58 1	236 3	235 0	1 004 6
Lake	150 4	17 2	89 9	165 7	423 1	508 8	53 7	197 7	535 9	1 296 1
Leelanau	28 4	20 9	49 4	124 6	223 4	97 4	70 0	151 3	421 9	740 7
Manistee	86 4	23 4	132 8	148 9	391 6	285 1	87 3	358 5	472 7	1 203 6
Mason	83 8	8 6	97 5	87 0	276 9	229 4	26 3	277 6	299 0	832 3
Mecosta	37 7	9 4	88 7	49 0	184 8	140 9	32 3	212 3	160 4	545 9
Midland	13 1	- -	111 4	61 6	186 1	62 5	- -	246 8	194 4	503 8
Missaukee	56 9	33 1	111 9	67 0	268 9	185 3	56 1	186 9	180 2	608 5
Montmorency	88 8	51 3	130 9	101 3	372 3	378 9	140 0	240 5	285 1	1 044 5
Newaygo	122 0	13 2	142 9	206 7	484 7	393 2	49 4	356 5	710 7	1 509 8
Oceana	67 6	15 5	108 6	95 9	287 6	198 3	50 7	272 8	305 0	826 8
Ogemaw	51 2	26 0	99 0	58 9	235 1	164 1	60 1	213 3	156 4	593 8
Osceola	28 9	15 9	106 9	72 4	224 2	87 0	58 7	238 4	244 3	628 4
Oscoda	117 1	19 8	83 8	78 8	299 5	415 4	37 9	125 0	264 1	842 5
Otsego	80 3	30 7	90 2	142 4	343 6	297 1	81 2	178 1	324 8	881 2
Presque Isle	48 2	115 6	120 7	56 7	341 2	208 0	238 4	242 9	138 1	827 4
Roscommon	48 3	45 0	80 4	82 3	255 9	214 2	98 4	129 3	242 1	684 0
Wexford	147 4	26 0	107 4	139 8	420 5	477 8	50 3	256 9	415 3	1 200 3
Total	2 189 3	1 017 9	3 458 1	3 151 7	9 816 9	7 649 6	2 635 1	7 897 8	9 167 5	27 350 1

(Table 59 continued on next page)

(Table 59 continued)

Southern Lower Peninsula [a]

Forest Survey Unit and county	Growing stock					Sawtimber				
	Major species group					Major species group				
	Pine	Other softwoods	Soft hardwoods	Hard hardwoods	All species	Pine	Other softwoods	Soft hardwoods	Hard hardwoods	All species
Allegan	41.1	2.8	102.6	124.4	270.8	142.5	6.0	331.7	434.1	914.3
Barry	8.2	8.6	53.3	100.4	170.4	35.4	32.9	136.1	376.6	581.1
Berrien	3.9	0.2	79.6	66.5	150.2	13.9	0.8	232.4	246.9	494.0
Branch	1.9	0.1	78.8	39.3	120.1	4.8	--	263.3	140.9	409.0
Calhoun	2.0	1.5	94.3	45.7	143.5	8.1	8.1	326.7	160.3	503.2
Cass	4.3	3.6	68.5	35.4	111.7	17.7	15.3	215.9	130.4	379.4
Clinton	0.4	--	21.6	25.8	47.8	2.3	--	55.5	85.2	143.0
Eaton	0.4	--	40.5	54.2	95.0	1.7	--	128.0	184.4	314.1
Genesee	0.0	0.0	45.7	56.1	101.9	--	--	124.6	175.3	299.9
Gratiot	6.4	--	24.7	27.8	58.9	14.7	--	61.4	75.1	151.2
Hillsdale	5.4	0.1	32.7	49.2	87.4	20.3	--	87.2	187.8	295.3
Huron	1.9	0.9	55.0	42.1	99.9	8.6	3.4	131.4	149.4	292.7
Ingham	0.5	0.0	43.2	27.6	71.3	0.7	--	121.9	93.2	215.8
Ionia	3.2	1.0	43.1	51.4	98.7	6.3	0.6	126.4	201.6	334.9
Jackson	3.4	1.2	87.4	101.8	193.8	12.9	1.3	281.5	400.3	696.1
Kalamazoo	23.3	6.3	77.5	84.2	191.4	108.8	19.4	241.5	305.4	675.2
Kent	15.5	4.8	87.0	102.6	209.9	46.0	16.9	244.6	345.2	652.8
Lapeer	15.9	5.5	71.9	84.1	177.4	64.1	16.4	183.7	301.2	565.3
Lenawee	0.3	0.9	54.8	48.8	104.8	1.1	2.3	168.0	180.6	352.0
Livingston	2.4	2.2	49.5	65.4	119.5	10.7	5.2	134.9	231.9	382.8
Macomb	0.0	1.9	28.0	24.1	54.0	--	6.5	71.9	60.5	138.9
Monroe	0.5	--	40.5	44.4	85.3	--	--	128.1	155.3	283.4
Montcalm	26.6	2.0	71.6	91.0	191.3	115.1	1.2	145.4	285.2	546.9
Muskegon	60.9	6.3	69.8	140.6	277.6	190.7	26.9	217.2	483.7	918.4
Oakland	2.9	2.4	68.9	91.1	165.3	14.4	8.7	217.1	347.2	587.3
Ottawa	23.9	1.3	62.8	68.6	156.5	95.2	4.8	180.0	252.7	532.6
Saginaw	15.4	0.5	81.4	45.2	142.5	56.7	1.7	196.3	134.5	389.2
St Clair	6.0	0.1	77.8	61.5	145.4	27.0	--	241.3	198.8	467.1
St Joseph	8.8	0.0	64.4	48.4	121.6	35.5	--	211.3	176.3	423.1
Sanilac	3.1	1.7	62.1	28.6	95.5	11.5	5.4	153.4	74.0	244.3
Shiawassee	0.8	0.5	28.8	25.8	56.0	2.5	2.5	90.5	91.1	186.6
Tuscola	13.5	4.3	77.1	44.1	138.9	47.1	10.2	159.4	142.5	359.2
Van Buren	8.4	7.2	89.8	81.0	186.4	27.1	36.1	285.8	294.1	643.1

(Table 59 continued on next page)

94

(Table 59 continued)

	Growing stock					Sawtimber				
	Major species group					Major species group				
Forest Survey Unit and county	Pine	Other softwoods	Soft hardwoods	Hard hardwoods	A species	Pine	Other softwoods	Soft hardwoods	Hard hardwoods	A species
Southern Lower Peninsula										
Washtenaw	4 7	1 4	48 2	91 1	145 4	20 9	5 2	139 0	343 5	508 5
Wayne	0 0	--	33 2	35 9	69 1	--	--	94 8	132 0	226 7
Total	315 8	69 5	2 116 0	2 154 3	4 655 6	1 164 0	237 9	6 128 3	7 577 2	15 107 4
A counties	3 785 7	4 943 6	9 488 3	9 085 6	27 303 2	14 440 0	14 877 4	22 839 2	26 734 5	78 891 0

All table cells without observations in the inventory sample are indicated by -- Table value of 0 0 indicates the volume rounds to less than 0 1 million cubic or board feet Columns and rows may not add to their totals due to rounding

95

Table 59a.—Net volume of growing-stock trees (at least 5 inches d.b.h.), in million cubic feet, and sawtimber trees, in million board feet (Doyle rule), on timberland by forest inventory unit, county, and major species group, Michigan, 2004

| Forest Survey Unit and county | Growing stock | | | | | Sawtimber | | | | |
| | Major species group | | | | | Major species group | | | | |
	Pine	Other softwoods	Soft hardwoods	Hard hardwoods	All species	Pine	Other softwoods	Soft hardwoods	Hard hardwoods	All species
Eastern Upper Peninsula unit a										
Alger	81.2	233.1	238.7	344.2	897.2	252.0	571.5	294.5	550.9	1 668.9
Chippewa	168.0	367.1	316.4	179.4	1 030.9	414.8	523.8	375.4	270.4	1 584.4
Delta	113.7	308.0	237.0	104.1	762.8	274.4	428.2	275.9	169.1	1 147.6
Luce	136.3	212.4	168.5	147.1	664.4	389.3	370.1	207.1	229.8	1 196.3
Mackinac	64.2	363.8	233.5	166.4	827.9	187.1	450.5	282.6	274.5	1 194.7
Menominee	45.2	273.7	199.1	146.1	664.2	157.6	308.5	213.1	183.4	862.5
Schoolcraft	154.4	203.0	172.8	92.8	623.0	382.1	264.5	212.7	166.9	1 026.2
Total	763.1	1 961.1	1 566.1	1 180.2	5 470.4	2 057.3	2 917.1	1 861.2	1 845.0	8 680.6
Western Upper Peninsula unit a										
Baraga	33.7	230.5	256.4	365.9	886.5	85.3	561.5	319.1	575.5	1 541.4
Dickinson	36.7	197.7	195.3	136.1	565.8	133.9	246.1	263.0	150.1	793.1
Gogebic	55.0	244.4	345.7	445.9	1 091.0	164.7	533.5	462.4	612.7	1 773.3
Houghton	61.4	217.1	299.9	365.5	943.9	206.2	578.5	389.9	595.5	1 770.0
Iron	89.5	211.6	289.3	364.5	954.8	302.0	351.9	334.6	548.6	1 537.2
Keweenaw	26.8	117.0	91.7	123.2	358.8	115.7	265.6	130.3	207.0	718.5
Marquette	163.8	459.3	445.4	424.2	1 492.7	513.6	877.6	501.8	666.2	2 559.1
Ontonagon	50.6	217.4	424.6	374.1	1 066.8	185.1	547.7	521.8	547.4	1 802.0
Total	517.5	1 895.2	2 348.1	2 599.4	7 360.3	1 706.4	3 962.4	2 923.0	3 903.0	12 494.7

(Table 59a continued on next page)

96

Northern Lower Pen nsu a

Forest Survey Un t and county	Grow ng stock — Major spec es group					Sawt mber — Major spec es group				
	P ne	Other softwoods	Soft hardwoods	Hard hardwoods	A spec es	P ne	Other softwoods	Soft hardwoods	Hard hardwoods	A spec es
Alcona	81 8	50 7	178 1	155 6	466 2	201 7	79 6	184 3	250 7	716 2
Alpena	51 9	77 8	126 3	59 5	315 5	155 6	91 7	133 8	96 9	478 1
Antrim	25 5	19 8	101 6	151 6	298 4	32 9	36 7	136 1	178 5	384 3
Arenac	14 2	3 8	79 0	40 4	137 5	38 4	7 1	104 9	69 7	220 1
Bay	1 7	1 3	39 9	13 8	56 7	6 9	2 2	54 2	33 1	96 4
Benzie	31 3	12 4	77 7	104 8	226 3	35 5	13 9	114 6	180 9	345 0
Charlevoix	28 5	69 2	96 3	131 0	324 9	92 7	105 6	150 1	187 9	536 2
Cheboygan	85 6	109 6	196 0	102 8	494 0	199 1	137 3	221 1	138 5	695 9
Clare	42 8	18 4	140 1	72 9	274 3	89 8	29 5	156 8	147 3	423 3
Crawford	119 3	20 7	59 5	96 8	296 3	253 4	17 6	48 7	137 6	457 3
Emmet	25 6	45 0	112 6	160 7	344 0	50 8	60 0	173 2	225 5	509 5
Gladwin	24 2	4 6	142 1	34 4	205 3	51 5	3 7	216 0	63 9	335 1
Grand Traverse	75 2	33 9	59 1	84 7	252 9	121 1	43 6	68 5	149 5	382 7
osco	157 3	46 1	114 5	57 9	375 8	330 5	53 7	181 3	95 8	661 3
sabella	13 7	6 4	73 7	43 4	137 1	22 0	7 8	123 9	80 4	234 2
Kalkaska	154 3	26 6	109 2	102 4	392 5	248 6	28 3	134 1	134 9	545 9
Lake	150 4	17 2	89 9	165 7	423 1	271 3	25 7	108 8	322 4	728 2
Leelanau	28 4	20 9	49 4	124 6	223 4	62 6	40 3	83 9	254 2	441 1
Manistee	86 4	23 4	132 8	148 9	391 6	166 7	44 2	230 7	294 3	735 9
Mason	83 8	8 6	97 5	87 0	276 9	113 0	14 0	169 1	189 3	485 4
Mecosta	37 7	9 4	88 7	49 0	184 8	84 9	17 3	119 8	96 9	318 9
Midland	13 1	--	111 4	61 6	186 1	51 0	--	129 9	117 6	298 4
Missaukee	56 9	33 1	111 9	67 0	268 9	99 3	23 9	99 6	101 8	324 6
Montmorency	88 8	51 3	130 9	101 3	372 3	265 8	69 4	126 8	156 4	618 5
Newaygo	122 0	13 2	142 9	206 7	484 7	203 6	25 9	221 7	441 4	892 6
Oceana	67 6	15 5	108 6	95 9	287 6	92 2	27 7	146 6	182 0	448 5
Ogemaw	51 2	26 0	99 0	58 9	235 1	100 5	29 0	121 8	92 6	343 9
Osceola	28 9	15 9	106 9	72 4	224 2	46 0	32 0	128 8	145 4	352 2
Oscoda	117 1	19 8	83 8	78 8	299 5	247 1	20 2	67 5	152 5	487 2
Otsego	80 3	30 7	90 2	142 4	343 6	175 8	39 3	90 3	178 4	483 8
Presque sle	48 2	115 6	120 7	56 7	341 2	131 4	106 4	131 4	72 0	441 3
Roscommon	48 3	45 0	80 4	82 3	255 9	134 5	44 1	66 2	130 7	375 5
Wexford	147 4	26 0	107 4	139 8	420 5	238 7	23 4	132 2	244 8	639 0
Tota	2 189 3	1 017 9	3 458 1	3 151 7	9 816 9	4 414 7	1 301 0	4 376 9	5 343 9	15 436 5

(Table 59a continued on next page)

Forest Survey Unit and county	Growing stock — Major species group					Sawtimber — Major species group				
	Pine	Other softwoods	Soft hardwoods	Hard hardwoods	All species	Pine	Other softwoods	Soft hardwoods	Hard hardwoods	All species
Southern Lower Peninsula										
Allegan	41 1	2 8	102 6	124 4	270 8	82 4	2 4	217 3	280 7	582 7
Barry	8 2	8 6	53 3	100 4	170 4	20 5	15 6	82 6	267 2	385 9
Berrien	3 9	0 2	79 6	66 5	150 2	6 5	0 4	137 9	164 9	309 7
Branch	1 9	0 1	78 8	39 3	120 1	1 8	- -	164 1	97 0	263 0
Calhoun	2 0	1 5	94 3	45 7	143 5	3 7	5 7	222 0	109 3	340 7
Cass	4 3	3 6	68 5	35 4	111 7	9 4	7 2	132 8	83 5	232 8
Clinton	0 4	- -	21 6	25 8	47 8	0 9	- -	31 4	66 6	98 9
Eaton	0 4	- -	40 5	54 2	95 0	1 0	- -	82 2	136 2	219 4
Genesee	0 0	0 0	45 7	56 1	101 9	- -	- -	76 1	114 7	190 8
Gratiot	6 4	- -	24 7	27 8	58 9	6 0	- -	33 5	41 6	81 1
Hillsdale	5 4	0 1	32 7	49 2	87 4	9 6	- -	51 1	126 2	186 9
Huron	1 9	0 9	55 0	42 1	99 9	3 9	1 8	86 1	111 0	202 7
Ingham	0 5	0 0	43 2	27 6	71 3	0 3	- -	70 3	72 9	143 6
Ionia	3 2	1 0	43 1	51 4	98 7	2 2	0 2	81 9	138 1	222 4
Jackson	3 4	1 2	87 4	101 8	193 8	5 5	0 5	175 6	272 3	453 9
Kalamazoo	23 3	6 3	77 5	84 2	191 4	61 4	9 5	146 5	204 2	421 6
Kent	15 5	4 8	87 0	102 6	209 9	23 8	8 8	158 8	207 8	399 2
Lapeer	15 9	5 5	71 9	84 1	177 4	41 3	7 9	105 9	206 2	361 3
Lenawee	0 3	0 9	54 8	48 8	104 8	0 4	1 0	109 5	121 5	232 4
Livingston	2 4	2 2	49 5	65 4	119 5	5 9	1 9	77 9	150 9	236 6
Macomb	0 0	1 9	28 0	24 1	54 0	- -	3 4	42 1	41 9	87 3
Monroe	0 5	- -	40 5	44 4	85 3	- -	- -	83 1	99 8	182 9
Montcalm	26 6	2 0	71 6	91 0	191 3	75 5	0 4	83 5	172 9	332 4
Muskegon	60 9	6 3	69 8	140 6	277 6	105 3	15 7	140 2	292 5	553 8
Oakland	2 9	2 4	68 9	91 1	165 3	9 9	4 2	157 8	237 4	409 3
Ottawa	23 9	1 3	62 8	68 6	156 5	49 8	2 4	106 5	172 5	331 1
Saginaw	15 4	0 5	81 4	45 2	142 5	34 8	0 7	120 5	89 4	245 3
St Clair	6 0	0 1	77 8	61 5	145 4	17 2	- -	179 3	124 0	320 5
St Joseph	8 8	0 0	64 4	48 4	121 6	17 4	- -	124 7	113 1	255 2
Sanilac	3 1	1 7	62 1	28 6	95 5	6 6	3 1	98 0	38 7	146 3
Shiawassee	0 8	0 5	28 8	25 8	56 0	1 3	1 2	56 7	58 4	117 6
Tuscola	13 5	4 3	77 1	44 1	138 9	21 8	4 6	87 9	97 7	212 0
Van Buren	8 4	7 2	89 8	81 0	186 4	11 9	25 7	185 9	194 4	417 9

(Table 59a continued on next page)

(Table 59a continued)

Forest Survey Unit and county	Growing stock					Sawtimber				
	Major species group					Major species group				
	Pine	Other softwoods	Soft hardwoods	Hard hardwoods	All species	Pine	Other softwoods	Soft hardwoods	Hard hardwoods	All species
Southern Lower Peninsula										
Washtenaw	4.7	1.4	48.2	911.1	1454	11.2	2.5	103.5	231.4	348.7
Wayne	0.0	--	33.2	35.9	69.1	--	--	61.6	102.0	163.6
Total	315.8	69.5	2 116.0	2 154.3	4 655.6	649.0	126.8	3 874.8	5 038.8	9 689.4
All counties	3 785.7	4 943.6	9 488.3	9 085.6	27 303.2	8 827.3	8 307.4	13 035.8	16 130.6	46 301.2

All table cells without observations in the inventory sample are indicated by -- Table value of 0.0 indicates the volume rounds to less than 0.1 million cubic or board feet Columns and rows may not add to their totals due to rounding

Table 60.—Average annual net growth of growing-stock trees (at least 5 inches d.b.h.), in million cubic feet, and sawtimber trees, in million board feet (International ¼-inch rule), on timberland by forest inventory unit, county, and major species group, Michigan, 1993 to 2004

Forest Survey Unit and county	Growing stock — Major species group					Sawtimber — Major species group				
	Pine	Other softwoods	Soft hardwoods	Hard hardwoods	All species	Pine	Other softwoods	Soft hardwoods	Hard hardwoods	All species
Eastern Upper Peninsula										
Alger	2.8	3.0	6.2	10.6	22.6	14.2	17.4	8.6	44.3	84.6
Chippewa	3.4	11.8	3.6	2.8	21.7	21.6	44.4	15.0	13.3	94.4
Delta	2.2	11.4	5.3	0.9	19.8	14.1	46.9	12.3	4.4	77.6
Luce	2.0	5.4	3.9	3.8	15.1	11.2	14.3	11.4	11.5	48.3
Mackinac	2.3	13.4	3.8	2.8	22.2	8.0	32.2	12.5	17.5	70.1
Menominee	1.5	9.7	5.3	4.8	21.4	1.3	27.4	11.9	18.0	58.6
Schoolcraft	5.0	4.9	1.4	1.4	12.8	21.3	13.7	3.8	7.4	46.2
Total	19.3	59.6	29.5	27.2	135.6	91.8	196.2	75.5	116.3	479.9
Western Upper Peninsula										
Baraga	0.4	4.0	4.2	6.7	15.2	0.6	7.8	10.8	22.1	41.3
Dickinson	0.2	7.6	11.4	1.1	20.3	1.1	23.4	18.3	5.2	48.0
Gogebic	1.2	4.7	8.6	12.2	26.7	5.7	21.9	25.5	46.0	99.1
Houghton	1.3	3.1	6.2	8.6	19.2	4.8	17.1	25.3	31.5	78.7
Iron	1.0	8.4	8.1	10.3	27.9	4.8	24.2	29.9	35.5	94.4
Keweenaw	0.2	0.0	0.1	0.8	1.2	1.4	0.3	-0.8	1.9	2.8
Marquette	6.0	13.3	11.4	7.2	37.8	28.8	44.8	36.0	22.7	132.3
Ontonagon	1.3	2.1	10.9	5.3	19.7	7.4	15.4	26.2	12.3	61.3
Total	11.5	43.3	61.0	52.1	168.0	54.5	154.9	171.1	177.2	557.8

(Table 60 continued on next page)

(Table 60 continued)

Forest Survey Unit and county	Growing stock — Major species group					Sawtimber — Major species group				
	Pine	Other softwoods	Soft hardwoods	Hard hardwoods	All species	Pine	Other softwoods	Soft hardwoods	Hard hardwoods	All species
Northern Lower Peninsula										
Alcona	3.1	0.9	5.4	3.7	13.0	5.7	2.2	20.6	19.9	48.4
Alpena	2.4	3.4	3.6	0.7	10.1	9.7	11.2	10.2	3.7	34.8
Antrim	0.5	0.8	1.4	0.7	3.3	4.0	1.3	2.0	4.2	11.4
Arenac	1.1	0.2	2.9	0.9	5.2	4.1	1.0	9.2	-0.3	14.0
Bay	--	--	1.1	--	1.1	--	--	6.6	--	6.6
Benzie	1.2	0.2	0.4	3.1	4.8	1.9	0.0	0.4	20.4	22.8
Charlevoix	1.2	0.3	1.6	3.5	6.5	4.8	2.7	8.7	11.7	27.9
Cheboygan	2.4	0.1	8.8	2.9	14.2	12.0	0.5	19.4	9.3	41.2
Clare	10.2	1.3	9.0	2.6	23.2	49.5	5.9	15.4	16.4	87.3
Crawford	2.9	-1.1	0.7	2.7	5.3	11.0	-6.4	2.2	11.1	17.9
Emmet	1.7	-1.6	1.7	6.3	8.0	9.8	1.9	4.0	27.4	43.1
Gladwin	3.8	--	6.8	1.0	11.6	10.8	--	27.2	1.7	39.7
Grand Traverse	8.3	1.4	-0.6	3.6	12.7	19.4	--	-3.7	10.5	26.1
Iosco	4.9	0.6	2.6	1.3	9.4	22.2	0.5	13.7	3.1	39.5
Isabella	0.8	--	2.3	1.5	4.6	2.7	--	7.0	5.1	14.8
Kalkaska	3.6	0.6	2.9	4.0	11.0	14.7	1.4	11.4	13.5	41.0
Lake	7.9	0.3	2.0	4.1	14.3	30.2	2.1	2.8	13.6	48.6
Leelanau	0.1	0.6	1.4	1.3	3.4	0.4	2.3	2.7	6.9	12.3
Manistee	2.8	-0.2	7.3	4.2	14.1	13.3	0.9	14.1	13.2	41.4
Mason	2.1	0.9	2.7	1.5	7.1	5.2	--	12.6	8.7	26.5
Mecosta	0.3	0.1	1.3	2.3	3.9	1.3	0.7	5.4	11.4	18.9
Midland	0.2	--	2.7	3.5	6.5	1.0	--	4.2	16.2	21.4
Missaukee	2.6	0.2	1.1	3.0	6.9	7.2	1.1	6.4	7.7	22.4
Montmorency	2.5	0.9	5.5	0.8	9.7	9.7	2.9	5.9	6.9	25.3
Newaygo	7.9	0.4	3.9	3.1	15.3	20.5	2.6	13.6	13.7	50.3
Oceana	1.4	0.3	4.5	2.1	8.3	7.7	2.1	17.3	6.3	33.4
Ogemaw	8.9	0.4	3.1	1.8	14.1	45.6	0.9	9.7	8.6	64.7
Osceola	2.4	0.2	4.1	0.7	7.4	3.6	--	6.5	0.9	11.0
Oscoda	4.0	0.3	2.5	2.2	9.0	12.6	2.5	3.8	15.3	34.3
Otsego	1.4	0.1	2.2	10.5	14.3	6.9	0.7	6.9	27.6	42.1
Presque Isle	0.1	1.3	3.5	0.5	5.4	0.2	1.1	4.5	3.3	9.2
Roscommon	0.2	0.0	-0.5	-1.1	-1.4	1.6	-1.2	7.0	4.3	11.8
Wexford	5.2	0.7	3.5	3.8	13.2	38.2	1.6	10.3	13.5	63.6
Total	98.2	13.8	101.1	82.5	295.6	387.4	42.1	288.1	335.9	1,053.6

(Table 60 continued on next page)

(Table 60 continued)

| | Growing stock | | | | | Sawtimber | | | | |
| | Major species group | | | | | Major species group | | | | |
Forest Survey Unit and county	Pine	Other softwoods	Soft hardwoods	Hard hardwoods	All species	Pine	Other softwoods	Soft hardwoods	Hard hardwoods	All species
Southern Lower Peninsula										
Allegan	1.2	--	7.7	5.9	14.8	13.7	--	21.5	16.6	51.7
Barry		0.0	0.3	2.4	2.7	--	--	1.4	10.1	11.5
Berrien	0.4	--	2.5	2.9	5.9	5.1	--	7.6	11.2	23.9
Branch	--	--	2.0	1.5	3.5	--	--	7.0	9.2	16.2
Calhoun	0.4	--	12.3	4.2	17.0	2.1	--	56.9	12.5	71.5
Cass	--	--	4.1	1.9	6.1	--	--	16.6	4.3	20.9
Clinton	--	--	2.0	0.4	2.4	--	--	2.7	--	2.7
Eaton	--	--	0.2	1.1	1.2	--	--	0.5	4.5	5.1
Genesee	--	--	1.6	2.0	3.6	--	--	3.8	6.0	9.8
Gratiot	0.0	--	0.3	1.1	1.4	--	--	1.1	7.8	8.9
Hillsdale	1.9	--	1.1	5.4	8.4	11.2	--	2.8	22.7	36.6
Huron	--	--	3.4	1.0	4.4	--	--	16.2	3.5	19.8
Ingham	--	--	0.7	1.3	2.0	--	--	1.7	8.5	10.2
Ionia	--	0.6	1.4	1.4	3.3	--	2.0	3.6	9.0	14.6
Jackson	0.2	0.0	2.3	2.7	5.3	1.8	--	9.4	15.4	26.6
Kalamazoo	2.0	--	7.5	2.6	12.1	10.7	--	27.9	10.0	48.6
Kent	0.7	--	3.7	2.5	7.0	2.3	--	13.4	7.7	23.4
Lapeer	1.5	0.3	1.0	1.2	4.0	5.8	2.3	3.3	6.1	17.5
Lenawee	--	--	4.1	1.7	5.8	--	--	16.9	6.4	23.4
Livingston	--	--	0.6	1.5	2.2	--	--	3.3	0.9	4.3
Macomb	--	0.1	2.5	0.8	3.4	--	0.3	4.2	1.9	6.4
Monroe	--	--	3.1	2.9	6.0	--	--	10.2	12.2	22.4
Montcalm	--	0.3	4.9	1.3	6.5	--	1.2	8.3	5.6	15.1
Muskegon	1.7	-0.2	1.3	4.2	7.0	9.7	-1.2	3.8	17.1	29.3
Oakland	0.9	--	0.5	0.9	2.2	4.7	--	-0.3	2.9	7.3
Ottawa	0.5	0.1	3.2	6.1	9.9	1.5	0.7	12.8	15.7	30.7
Saginaw	0.7	--	2.6	2.4	5.7	1.6	--	8.7	3.5	13.8
Sanilac	1.0	0.3	0.1	1.4	2.8	3.8	1.7	1.6	1.7	8.8
Shiawassee	--	--	1.7	0.1	1.8	--	--	0.3	0.6	0.9
St. Clair	0.0	--	1.0	0.9	1.8	0.3	--	2.9	2.9	6.1
St. Joseph	0.1	--	2.8	2.0	4.9	0.5	--	9.7	12.6	22.8
Tuscola	--	0.4	2.1	2.8	5.4	--	1.9	6.3	7.8	16.0
Van Buren	0.2	--	2.4	1.8	4.3	1.1	--	6.1	8.9	16.1

(Table 60 continued on next page)

(Table 60 continued)

	Growing stock					Sawtimber				
		Major species group					Major species group			
Forest Survey Unit and county	Pine	Other softwoods	Soft hardwoods	Hard hardwoods	All species	Pine	Other softwoods	Soft hardwoods	Hard hardwoods	All species
Southern Lower Peninsula										
Washtenaw	--	0.0	1.7	4.0	5.8	--	--	8.0	18.4	26.3
Wayne	--	--	1.2	5.8	7.0	--	--	8.3	24.1	32.4
Total	13.4	2.0	90.1	82.2	187.6	75.7	8.9	308.4	308.4	701.4
All counties	142.4	118.8	281.6	244.0	786.8	609.5	402.2	843.1	937.9	2,792.7

All table cells without observations in the inventory sample are indicated by -- Table value of 0.0 indicates the volume rounds to less than 0.1 million cubic or board feet. Columns and rows may not add to their totals due to rounding.

103

Table 61.—Average annual removals of growing-stock trees (at least 5 inches d.b.h.), in million cubic feet, and sawtimber trees, in million board feet (International ¼-inch rule), on timberland by forest inventory unit, county, and major species group, Michigan, 1993 to 2004

Forest Survey Unit and county	Growing stock					Sawtimber				
	Major species group					Major species group				
	Pine	Other softwoods	Soft hardwoods	Hard hardwoods	All species	Pine	Other softwoods	Soft hardwoods	Hard hardwoods	All species
Eastern Upper Peninsula [a]										
Alger	1 8	3 3	3 6	3 8	12 5	9 7	8 1	8 9	14 7	41 4
Chippewa	2 6	0 7	0 7	- -	4 0	9 2	0 7	1 6	- -	11 4
Delta	0 6	2 7	3 1	0 9	7 3	1 2	8 4	3 0	0 6	13 2
Luce	1 0	1 7	2 0	1 7	6 4	4 6	9 6	6 4	5 4	26 1
Mackinac	0 3	2 3	3 6	0 6	6 8	1 6	8 3	13 9	2 4	26 2
Menominee	0 4	3 1	4 5	4 6	12 6	2 0	11 3	11 4	16 9	41 6
Schoolcraft	1 3	1 3	2 5	2 0	7 1	4 9	3 3	9 6	5 4	23 2
Total	8 0	15 2	20 0	13 5	56 7	33 2	49 7	54 8	45 4	183 2
Western Upper Peninsula [a]										
Baraga	- -	- -	4 8	2 4	7 3	- -	- -	18 1	9 9	28 0
Dickinson	0 1	2 6	3 5	0 1	6 4	0 6	9 4	7 8	0 6	18 4
Gogebic	- -	0 1	7 6	3 4	11 2	- -	0 7	20 0	13 0	33 7
Houghton	0 4	1 0	2 3	6 1	9 8	1 6	2 4	10 1	22 1	36 3
Iron	0 1	2 0	5 3	2 6	10 1	0 7	6 1	14 5	7 2	28 5
Keweenaw	- -	- -	0 7	- -	0 7	- -	- -	- -	- -	- -
Marquette	4 5	9 9	9 4	4 9	28 7	17 7	31 3	19 3	2 2	70 5
Ontonagon	- -	1 0	4 3	1 9	7 2	- -	4 4	11 9	5 9	22 2
Total	5 2	16 5	38 1	21 5	81 3	20 5	54 4	101 7	61 0	237 6

(Table 61 continued on next page)

104

(Table 61 continued)

Forest Survey Unit and county	Growing stock — Major species group					Sawtimber — Major species group				
	Pine	Other softwoods	Soft hardwoods	Hard hardwoods	All species	Pine	Other softwoods	Soft hardwoods	Hard hardwoods	All species
Northern Lower Peninsula										
Alcona	--	--	6.8	5.8	12.6	--	--	16.0	20.8	36.8
Alpena	--	0.3	1.1	--	1.4	--	1.6	4.4	--	6.0
Antrim	0.2	--	0.1	--	0.3	0.9	--	0.5	--	1.4
Arenac	--	0.3	4.1	--	4.3	--	1.5	7.6	--	9.1
Benzie	0.5	--	--	1.1	1.6	--	--	--	4.9	4.9
Charlevoix	--	--	1.5	0.3	1.8	--	--	6.9	1.6	8.5
Cheboygan	0.2	--	1.5	0.3	2.0	--	--	1.4	1.4	2.7
Clare	--	--	1.4	0.8	2.2	--	--	5.3	3.3	8.6
Crawford	--	--	0.5	0.3	0.8	--	--	2.4	--	2.4
Emmet	1.8	--	0.3	0.1	2.2	3.8	--	--	--	3.8
Gladwin	1.1	--	1.0	0.4	2.4	5.4	--	3.1	2.1	10.5
Grand Traverse	3.0	--	1.1	1.0	5.1	1.1	--	3.6	2.9	7.6
Iosco	0.8	--	--	0.1	0.9	1.5	--	--	0.4	1.8
Isabella	--	--	0.3	2.1	2.4	--	--	--	9.0	9.0
Kalkaska	0.9	0.8	0.7	2.1	4.5	4.1	1.2	2.0	7.3	14.6
Lake	5.9	--	1.1	1.4	8.4	21.0	--	1.3	5.6	27.9
Leelanau	--	--	--	0.3	0.3	--	--	--	1.5	1.5
Manistee	2.2	--	0.5	2.1	4.7	5.0	--	1.6	9.3	15.9
Mason	4.1	1.2	0.3	--	5.6	11.7	--	1.4	--	13.1
Mecosta	0.6	--	0.3	0.3	1.2	2.8	--	1.5	1.3	5.5
Midland	--	--	0.6	--	0.6	--	--	3.0	--	3.0
Missaukee	0.2	0.1	1.7	0.8	2.9	0.9	0.7	4.3	2.0	7.8
Montmorency	--	--	1.2	--	1.2	--	--	1.4	--	1.4
Newaygo	0.7	--	0.9	2.9	4.6	--	--	2.1	13.8	15.9
Oceana	1.9	--	--	--	1.9	7.8	--	--	--	7.8
Ogemaw	3.2	--	12.0	2.7	17.9	6.2	--	26.9	9.7	42.9
Osceola	0.2	--	3.7	0.4	3.9	--	--	4.2	--	4.2
Oscoda	0.3	--	1.3	0.4	2.0	0.5	--	5.6	--	6.1
Otsego	1.5	--	0.2	3.0	4.8	3.7	--	0.5	7.4	11.7
Presque Isle	0.1	1.2	2.0	0.2	3.5	0.8	4.8	1.8	--	7.4
Roscommon	0.4	--	--	0.1	0.5	2.0	--	--	0.5	2.5
Wexford	4.8	--	0.1	0.7	5.6	9.1	--	--	1.8	10.9
Total	34.6	3.8	46.4	29.4	114.3	88.3	9.8	108.9	106.3	313.3

(Table 61 continued on next page)

(Table 61 continued)

Southern Lower Peninsula

Forest Survey Unit and county	Growing stock					Sawtimber				
	Major species group					Major species group				
	Pine	Other softwoods	Soft hardwoods	Hard hardwoods	All species	Pine	Other softwoods	Soft hardwoods	Hard hardwoods	All species
Allegan	--	--	3.1	1.5	4.6	--	--	3.8	3.9	7.7
Berrien	--	--	0.9	0.6	1.5	--	--	4.5	3.2	7.6
Branch	--	--	2.7	0.6	3.3	--	--	10.7	2.9	13.6
Calhoun	--	--	0.3	--	0.3	--	--	1.2	--	1.2
Cass	--	--	0.4	1.7	2.0	--	--	1.9	8.2	10.1
Genesee	--	--	0.5	--	0.5	--	--	1.3	--	1.3
Hillsdale	--	--	0.3	--	0.3	--	--	--	--	--
Huron	--	--	1.5	0.5	2.1	--	--	5.9	2.5	8.4
Ionia	--	--	1.0	1.2	2.2	--	--	4.8	6.6	11.5
Jackson	--	--	--	0.7	0.7	--	--	--	3.4	3.4
Kalamazoo	4.6	--	0.4	--	5.0	21.4	--	--	--	21.4
Lapeer	--	--	0.5	0.2	0.8	--	--	1.2	1.1	2.3
Lenawee	--	--	--	0.8	0.8	--	--	--	3.9	3.9
Livingston	--	--	1.0	1.0	1.9	--	--	4.2	4.6	8.8
Macomb	--	--	0.6	0.3	0.9	--	--	1.0	1.3	2.4
Oakland	--	--	0.3	0.2	0.5	--	--	1.0	1.1	2.1
Ottawa	--	--	--	0.1	0.1	--	--	--	--	--
Saginaw	--	--	2.0	0.5	2.5	--	--	7.6	2.4	10.0
St Joseph	--	--	2.4	1.2	3.6	--	--	8.5	5.4	13.9
Tuscola	--	--	0.3	--	0.3	--	--	1.3	--	1.3
Van Buren	--	--	1.2	3.6	4.8	--	--	6.0	17.0	23.0
Wayne	--	--	--	0.4	0.4	--	--	--	2.2	2.2
Total	4.6	--	19.3	15.1	39.0	21.4	--	65.0	69.6	156.1
All counties	52.4	35.5	123.8	79.5	291.2	163.5	113.9	330.5	282.3	890.2

All table cells without observations in the inventory sample are indicated by -- . Table value of 0.0 indicates the volume rounds to less than 0.1 million cubic or board feet. Columns and rows may not add to their totals due to rounding.

Table 61a.—Average annual removals of growing-stock trees (at least 5 inches d.b.h.), in million cubic feet, and sawtimber trees, in million board feet (Doyle rule), on timberland by forest inventory unit, county, and major species group, Michigan, 1993 to 2004

Forest Survey Unit and county	Growing stock — Major species group					Sawtimber — Major species group				
	Pine	Other softwoods	Soft hardwoods	Hard hardwoods	All species	Pine	Other softwoods	Soft hardwoods	Hard hardwoods	All species
Eastern Upper Peninsula										
Alger	1.8	3.3	3.6	3.8	12.5	6.1	3.7	4.2	8.9	22.9
Chippewa	2.6	0.7	0.7	--	4.0	3.9	0.4	0.9	--	5.2
Delta	0.6	2.7	3.1	0.9	7.3	0.6	3.4	1.2	0.2	5.4
Luce	1.0	1.7	2.0	1.7	6.4	3.1	7.8	3.1	3.0	17.0
Mackinac	0.3	2.3	3.6	0.6	6.8	0.6	5.6	9.0	1.0	16.1
Menominee	0.4	3.1	4.5	4.6	12.6	1.3	3.9	5.5	10.6	21.3
Schoolcraft	1.3	1.3	2.5	2.0	7.1	1.9	1.9	5.6	2.8	12.1
Total	8.0	15.2	20.0	13.5	56.7	17.6	26.6	29.3	26.5	100.0
Western Upper Peninsula										
Baraga	--	--	4.8	2.4	7.3	--	--	10.4	6.3	16.7
Dickinson	0.1	2.6	3.5	0.1	6.4	0.3	4.2	4.1	0.4	9.0
Gogebic	--	0.1	7.6	3.4	11.2	--	0.5	7.7	7.7	15.8
Houghton	0.4	1.0	2.3	6.1	9.8	0.3	1.0	5.0	14.4	20.8
Iron	0.1	2.0	5.3	2.6	10.1	0.5	3.4	6.7	4.2	14.8
Keweenaw	--	--	0.7	--	0.7	--	--	--	--	--
Marquette	4.5	9.9	9.4	4.9	28.7	10.3	14.5	9.7	1.2	35.6
Ontonagon	--	1.0	4.3	1.9	7.2	--	2.8	4.4	3.5	10.8
Total	5.2	16.5	38.1	21.5	81.3	11.4	26.4	48.0	37.6	123.5

(Table 61a continued on next page)

(Table 61a continued)

Northern Lower Peninsula

Forest Survey Unit and county	Growing stock — Major species group					Sawtimber — Major species group				
	Pine	Other softwoods	Soft hardwoods	Hard hardwoods	All species	Pine	Other softwoods	Soft hardwoods	Hard hardwoods	All species
Alcona	- -	- -	6 8	5 8	12 6	- -	- -	6 6	10 3	16 9
Alpena	- -	0 3	1 1	- -	1 4	- -	1 1	2 1	- -	3 3
Antrim	0 2	- -	0 1	- -	0 3	- -	- -	0 3	- -	0 3
Arenac	- -	0 3	4 1	- -	4 3	- -	0 8	3 8	- -	4 6
Benzie	0 5	- -	- -	1 1	1 6	- -	- -	- -	2 4	2 4
Charlevoix	- -	- -	1 5	0 3	1 8	- -	- -	3 7	0 9	4 6
Cheboygan	0 2	- -	1 5	0 3	2 0	- -	- -	- -	- -	- -
Clare	- -	- -	1 4	0 8	2 2	- -	- -	1 5	2 0	3 5
Crawford	- -	- -	0 5	0 3	0 8	- -	- -	1 3	- -	1 3
Emmet	1 8	- -	0 3	0 1	2 2	1 0	- -	- -	- -	1 0
Gladwin	1 1	- -	1 0	0 4	2 4	2 8	- -	1 3	2 3	6 4
Grand Traverse	3 0	- -	1 1	1 0	5 1	0 4	- -	2 0	1 7	4 1
Iosco	0 8	- -	- -	0 1	0 9	0 7	- -	- -	0 1	0 9
Isabella	- -	- -	0 3	2 1	2 4	- -	- -	- -	5 5	5 5
Kalkaska	0 9	0 8	0 7	2 1	4 5	2 4	0 4	0 9	4 3	8 0
Lake	5 9	- -	1 1	1 4	8 4	7 4	- -	0 5	3 7	11 6
Leelanau	- -	- -	- -	0 3	0 3	- -	- -	- -	1 1	1 1
Manistee	2 2	- -	0 5	2 1	4 7	1 8	- -	1 1	5 8	8 7
Mason	4 1	1 2	0 3	- -	5 6	4 8	- -	0 8	- -	5 6
Mecosta	0 6	- -	0 3	0 3	1 2	2 1	- -	0 7	0 6	3 5
Midland	- -	- -	0 6	- -	0 6	- -	- -	1 8	- -	1 8
Missaukee	0 2	0 1	1 7	0 8	2 9	0 8	0 4	2 1	0 8	4 2
Montmorency	- -	- -	1 2	- -	1 2	- -	- -	0 8	- -	0 8
Newaygo	0 7	- -	0 9	2 9	4 6	- -	- -	1 3	8 4	9 7
Oceana	1 9	- -	- -	- -	1 9	4 1	- -	- -	- -	4 1
Ogemaw	3 2	- -	12 0	2 7	17 9	2 5	- -	11 8	5 2	19 4
Osceola	0 2	- -	3 7	- -	3 9	- -	- -	2 5	- -	2 5
Oscoda	0 3	- -	1 3	0 4	2 0	0 2	- -	2 0	- -	2 2
Otsego	1 5	- -	0 2	3 0	4 8	2 9	- -	0 2	4 2	7 4
Presque Isle	0 1	1 2	2 0	0 2	3 5	0 6	2 2	0 8	- -	3 5
Roscommon	0 4	- -	- -	0 1	0 5	0 7	- -	- -	0 2	0 9
Wexford	4 8	- -	0 1	0 7	5 6	2 5	- -	- -	1 1	3 6
Total	34 6	3 8	46 4	29 4	114 3	37 5	5 0	49 7	60 8	153 0

Forest Survey Unit and county	Growing stock					Sawtimber				
	Major species group					Major species group				
	Pine	Other softwoods	Soft hardwoods	Hard hardwoods	All species	Pine	Other softwoods	Soft hardwoods	Hard hardwoods	All species
Southern Lower Peninsula										
Allegan	--	--	3.1	1.5	4.6	--	--	1.7	2.7	4.4
Berrien	--	--	0.9	0.6	1.5	--	--	3.1	2.6	5.6
Branch	--	--	2.7	0.6	3.3	--	--	7.6	2.0	9.6
Calhoun	--	--	0.3	--	0.3	--	--	0.6	--	0.6
Cass	--	--	0.4	1.7	2.0	--	--	1.6	6.0	7.6
Genesee	--	--	0.5	--	0.5	--	--	0.8	--	0.8
Hillsdale	--	--	0.3	--	0.3	--	--	--	--	--
Huron	--	--	1.5	0.5	2.1	--	--	3.6	1.5	5.0
onia	--	--	1.0	1.2	2.2	--	--	3.4	5.5	8.9
Jackson	--	--	--	0.7	0.7	--	--	--	2.2	2.2
Kalamazoo	4.6	--	0.4	--	5.0	13.9	--	--	--	13.9
Lapeer	--	--	0.5	0.2	0.8	--	--	0.5	1.0	1.5
Lenawee	--	--	--	0.8	0.8	--	--	--	3.4	3.4
Livingston	--	--	1.0	1.0	1.9	--	--	2.1	2.9	5.0
Macomb	--	--	0.6	0.3	0.9	--	--	0.6	1.1	1.7
Oakland	--	--	0.3	0.2	0.5	--	--	0.5	1.0	1.6
Ottawa	--	--	--	0.1	0.1	--	--	--	--	--
Saginaw	--	--	2.0	0.5	2.5	--	--	4.6	1.6	6.2
St Joseph	--	--	2.4	1.2	3.6	--	--	6.3	3.0	9.3
Tuscola	--	--	0.3	--	0.3	--	--	1.1	--	1.1
Van Buren	--	--	1.2	3.6	4.8	--	--	3.9	11.6	15.6
Wayne	--	--	--	0.4	0.4	--	--	--	2.5	2.5
Total	4.6	--	19.3	15.1	39.0	13.9	--	41.8	50.6	106.4
All counties	52.4	35.5	123.8	79.5	291.2	80.4	58.0	168.9	175.6	482.9

All table cells without observations in the inventory sample are indicated by — Table value of 0 0 indicates the volume rounds to less than 0 1 million cubic or board feet Columns and rows may not add to their totals due to rounding

Table 65.—Sampling errors, in percent, for net volume, average annual net growth, average annual removals, and average annual mortality on timberland, and forest and timberland area by forest inventory unit and county, Michigan, 2004

Forest Survey Unit and county	Forest area	Timberland area	Growing stock				Sawtimber			
			Volume	Average annual net growth	Average annual removals	Average annual mortality	Volume	Average annual net growth	Average annual removals	Average annual mortality
Eastern Upper Peninsula										
Alger	5.73	5.81	6.83	23.79	31.52	35.01	7.99	22.55	30.86	39.80
Chippewa	4.47	4.55	5.74	16.58	64.73	21.91	6.75	19.19	86.49	29.72
Delta	5.26	5.30	6.67	21.13	34.71	25.57	7.98	18.34	41.17	32.91
Luce	5.87	5.97	7.23	24.70	59.05	29.53	8.23	21.93	71.10	33.47
Mackinac	5.43	5.56	6.75	28.70	32.67	29.20	7.81	26.80	34.95	39.90
Menominee	5.72	5.73	7.26	28.67	36.37	30.04	9.39	20.34	37.83	38.88
Schoolcraft	5.49	5.59	7.57	25.82	53.99	30.72	9.06	20.93	63.08	44.79
Total	0.66	0.75	1.66	6.90	15.38	10.23	2.32	7.64	18.17	18.17
Western Upper Peninsula										
Baraga	5.75	5.83	6.77	29.95	30.32	30.35	7.61	25.10	32.42	32.27
Dickinson	6.54	6.54	8.14	31.16	45.43	29.09	9.65	26.60	48.93	38.91
Gogebic	5.00	5.19	5.94	18.19	32.98	20.42	6.93	16.74	31.50	28.06
Houghton	5.74	5.84	6.71	20.13	28.91	40.40	7.61	18.49	31.04	41.22
Iron	5.09	5.12	6.15	20.70	31.77	22.44	7.18	16.70	36.73	33.58
Keweenaw	7.43	9.70	10.86	76.16	82.88	51.77	12.10	56.98	- -	67.91
Marquette	3.88	3.95	5.05	19.14	22.23	18.40	6.19	17.14	23.43	21.26
Ontonagon	4.71	4.95	5.97	27.21	38.80	23.86	7.10	23.77	44.59	33.86
Total	0.52	0.73	1.43	6.08	11.18	8.36	2.00	7.18	11.75	11.75

(Table 65 continued on next page)

(Table 65 continued)

Forest Survey Unit and county	Forest area	Timber land area	Growing stock				Sawtimber			
			Volume	Average annual net growth	Average annual removals	Average annual mortality	Volume	Average annual net growth	Average annual removals	Average annual mortality
Northern Lower Peninsula										
Alcona	7.62	7.65	9.2	25.6	34.3	46.4	10.7	30.3	37.4	48.5
Alpena	8.41	8.48	10.8	29.7	91.3	49.1	13.5	28.4	98.7	58.0
Antrim	10.2	10.2	11.7	42.6	72.0	38.7	13.8	50.9	71.3	95.9
Arenac	13.41	13.53	17.4	59.1	66.0	37.5	21.0	42.7	60.1	39.0
Bay	22.59	22.59	26.8	94.6	--	74.4	30.9	94.6	--	--
Benzie	11.73	11.98	14.2	50.9	63.0	69.4	16.3	38.9	84.2	85.9
Charlevoix	10.44	10.44	11.7	41.7	72.4	44.0	12.7	45.9	72.1	71.9
Cheboygan	7.11	7.17	8.9	29.9	81.2	37.1	10.3	37.9	85.9	73.6
Clare	9.95	9.96	12.2	57.1	97.9	46.4	14.3	47.5	100.0	66.3
Crawford	7.92	8.07	10.4	62.0	60.8	53.5	12.0	52.4	85.9	62.0
Emmet	9.41	9.45	11.1	73.6	55.4	52.1	12.6	91.6	65.9	56.4
Gladwin	9.87	9.92	13.4	32.6	75.8	37.2	16.3	35.7	75.4	100.0
Grand Traverse	10.23	10.46	12.5	88.1	48.2	74.4	14.6	63.1	60.4	74.4
Iosco	8.5	8.61	10.9	25.9	100.0	44.8	13.1	23.8	99.6	54.5
Isabella	13.41	13.41	17.6	56.6	74.1	97.8	20.8	57.2	86.3	100.0
Kalkaska	7.92	8.02	9.9	34.5	50.7	42.0	11.3	30.1	52.2	85.9
Lake	7.77	7.77	9.6	24.8	51.5	37.3	11.1	23.6	57.6	100.0
Leelanau	11.69	12.91	15.3	53.0	86.3	55.9	16.6	50.8	86.3	62.7
Manistee	8.7	8.74	10.7	31.6	49.5	77.5	12.1	38.8	47.6	96.0
Mason	10.22	10.37	12.3	44.3	65.5	52.5	14.0	48.1	77.5	64.1
Mecosta	11.98	12.06	15.2	60.8	74.2	73.0	18.0	79.0	81.6	78.0
Midland	11.1	11.1	14.1	70.4	85.9	85.9	16.7	64.3	85.9	--
Missaukee	9.06	9.09	10.8	36.2	64.6	66.1	13.1	36.5	68.5	75.6
Montmorency	7.94	8.06	10.2	35.4	60.2	51.8	12.4	32.9	86.3	67.3
Newaygo	7.57	7.57	9.0	25.3	46.8	31.8	10.1	31.3	53.6	34.3
Oceana	10.2	10.31	12.4	33.2	94.4	43.3	14.0	34.2	100.0	94.7
Ogemaw	9.13	9.17	11.6	36.9	43.6	39.3	12.8	32.5	47.6	66.0
Osceola	10.7	10.7	13.4	44.9	45.1	53.7	15.2	35.1	74.4	--
Oscoda	7.59	7.86	10.4	34.1	55.4	32.7	12.5	38.6	69.2	44.1
Otsego	8.62	8.65	10.3	32.4	41.6	57.1	11.8	29.6	61.5	93.7
Presque Isle	7.74	7.8	10.2	69.0	54.1	49.0	12.0	61.1	60.2	66.0
Roscommon	8.3	8.38	11.2	83.5	61.4	49.5	13.2	0.0	61.6	54.5
Wexford	8.46	8.49	10.3	33.1	65.1	45.4	12.2	30.6	71.2	63.2
Total	0.61	0.65	1.3	7.2	11.7	9.2	1.8	7.6	13.1	13.1

(Table 65 continued on next page)

(Table 65 continued)

Forest Survey Unit and county	Forest area	Timber land area	Growing stock				Sawtimber			
			Volume	Average annual net growth	Average annual removals	Average annual mortality	Volume	Average annual net growth	Average annual removals	Average annual mortality
Southern Lower Peninsula										
A egan	10.23	10.29	13.4	29.2	77.3	39.0	15.4	26.827	56.9	69.9
Barry	12.4	12.4	15.1	53.9	- -	56.2	17.2	47.177	- -	100.0
Berr en	14.05	14.21	17.2	39.3	93.2	47.2	17.8	44.643	93.2	57.0
Branch	16.44	16.44	19.5	49.2	79.0	100.0	22.1	50.473	91.8	- -
Ca houn	15.38	15.6	18.2	69.8	100.0	50.7	20.1	67.029	100.0	- -
Cass	15.39	15.39	18.5	49.3	93.2	57.5	20.1	44.67	93.2	53.7
C nton	22.47	22.47	26.7	66.1	- -	85.6	35.0	110.786	- -	100.0
Eaton	18.65	18.65	22.4	66.6	- -	93.2	26.0	68.648	- -	93.2
Genesee	15.19	15.19	21.0	58.2	73.4	48.9	24.7	44.77	93.2	71.2
Grat ot	21.01	21.01	25.6	75.0	- -	97.7	29.2	68.335	- -	- -
H sda e	17.2	17.2	19.7	62.1	93.2	57.2	21.9	53.356	- -	81.4
Huron	16.62	16.62	21.9	47.8	88.8	71.0	27.5	50.465	86.8	100.0
Ingham	18.03	18.03	23.1	53.2	- -	69.1	26.0	44.349	- -	68.6
Ion a	16.72	16.72	22.9	44.2	93.2	72.9	27.0	46.928	93.2	69.4
Jackson	12.47	12.56	16.3	37.1	71.9	59.5	17.7	37.136	72.1	76.7
Ka amazoo	13.25	13.25	16.3	46.9	100.0	47.4	17.8	47.497	100.0	78.1
Kent	11.04	11.04	13.0	32.6	- -	48.4	14.4	35.925	- -	69.6
Lapeer	12.29	12.29	15.4	46.6	79.9	60.4	18.0	61.898	77.6	92.8
Lenawee	15.5	15.5	17.8	87.9	97.7	- -	19.7	81.138	97.7	- -
L v ngston	14.54	14.54	17.3	68.1	100.0	66.4	18.8	75.581	100.0	76.3
Macomb	21.23	21.23	26.8	55.7	83.1	93.2	34.2	49.074	100.0	- -
Monroe	20.47	20.47	23.2	44.6	- -	93.2	25.0	47.621	- -	- -
Montca m	11.17	11.17	13.6	61.4	- -	76.4	16.2	37.398	- -	95.0
Muskegon	10.31	10.31	12.3	51.5	- -	60.3	13.7	50.009	- -	65.2
Oak and	12.83	12.94	16.5	99.7	68.6	47.6	18.5	76.797	69.0	54.6
Ottawa	14.02	14.02	17.0	52.7	100.0	73.5	18.8	44.476	- -	73.6
Sag naw	14.36	14.36	15.7	47.0	82.2	63.2	17.5	41.044	77.5	79.4
San ac	13.79	13.79	17.8	56.3	- -	93.3	19.9	68.46	- -	100.0
Sh awassee	16.63	16.76	19.8	40.0	70.3	60.0	21.7	36.777	78.7	69.0
St. C a r	15.02	15.02	19.1	61.1	- -	55.7	21.3	47.988	- -	83.2
St. Joseph	19.04	19.04	24.2	100.5	- -	89.7	25.8	102.522	- -	100.0
Tusco a	12.83	12.83	15.7	60.9	100.0	57.1	19.1	43.415	100.0	74.6
Van Buren	12.04	12.04	14.7	49.6	73.7	81.1	16.1	44.426	73.5	81.0

(Table 65 continued on next page)

(Table 65 continued)

Forest Survey Unit and county	Forest area	Timber land area	Growing stock				Sawtimber			
			Volume	Average annual net growth	Average annual removals	Average annual mortality	Volume	Average annual net growth	Average annual removals	Average annual mortality
Southern Lower Peninsula										
Washtenaw	13.21	13.21	17.0	52.2	- -	100.0	19.5	53.175	- -	- -
Wayne	19.89	19.89	26.6	95.1	97.7	77.4	30.5	103.226	97.7	97.7
Total	1.45	1.46	2.2	10.0	23.4	10.8	2.7	11.3	24.5	24.5
All counties	0.37	0.41	0.8	4.0	7.1	4.9	1.1	4.5	8.0	6.8

Sampling errors that exceed 100% are reported as 100%. The sampling error is not calculated when the estimated value is equal to 0 and is indicated by --

www.ingramcontent.com/pod-product-compliance
Lightning Source LLC
Chambersburg PA
CBHW081222280526
45787CB00006B/2485